Anthony Horowitz

WHO WROTE THAT?

WHO WROTE THAT?

Anthony Horowitz

Dennis Abrams

Foreword by
Kyle Zimmer

CHELSEA HOUSE
PUBLISHERS
An imprint of Infobase Publishing

Anthony Horowitz

Copyright © 2006 by Infobase Publishing

All rights reserved. No part of this book may be reproduced or utilized in any form by any means, electronic or mechanical, including photocopying, recording, or by any information storage or retrieval systems, without permission in writing from the publisher. For information contact:

Chelsea House
An imprint of Infobase Publishing
132 West 31st Street
New York NY 10001

Library of Congress Cataloging-in-Publication Data

Abrams, Dennis, 1960–
  Anthony Horowitz / Dennis Abrams.
    p. cm. — (Who wrote that?)
  Includes bibliographical references and index.
  ISBN 0-7910-8968-1
  1. Horowitz, Anthony, 1955—Juvenile literature. 2. Authors, English—20th century—
Biography—Juvenile literature. 3. Children's stories—Authorship—Juvenile literature. I.
Title. II. Series.
  PR6058.O715Z53 2005
  823'.914—dc22   2005030090

Chelsea House books are available at special discounts when purchased in bulk quantities for businesses, associations, institutions, or sales promotions. Please call our Special Sales Department in New York at (212) 967-8800 or (800) 322-8755.

You can find Chelsea House on the World Wide Web at http://www.chelseahouse.com

Text and cover design by Keith Trego

Printed in the United States of America

Bang EJB 10 9 8 7 6 5 4 3 2 1

This book is printed on acid-free paper.

All links and Web addresses were checked and verified to be correct at the time of publication. Because of the dynamic nature of the Web, some addresses and links may have changed since publication and may no longer be valid.

Table of Contents

FOREWORD BY
KYLE ZIMMER
PRESIDENT, FIRST BOOK

HUMANITY IS POWERED by stories. From our earliest days as thinking beings, we employed every available tool to tell each other stories. We danced, drew pictures on the walls of our caves, spoke, and sang. All of this extraordinary effort was designed to entertain, recount the news of the day, explain natural occurrences—and then gradually to build religious and cultural traditions and establish the common bonds and continuity that eventually formed civilizations. Stories are the most powerful force in the universe; they are the primary element that has distinguished our evolutionary path.

Our love of the story has not diminished with time. Enormous segments of societies are devoted to the art of storytelling. Book sales in the United States alone topped $26 billion last year; movie studios spend fortunes to create and promote stories; and the news industry is more pervasive in its presence than ever before.

There is no mystery to our fascination. Great stories are magic. They can introduce us to new cultures, or remind us of the nobility and failures of our own, inspire us to greatness or scare us to death; but above all, stories provide human insight on a level that is unavailable through any other source. In fact, stories connect each of us to the rest of humanity not just in our own time, but also throughout history.

This special magic of books is the greatest treasure that we can hand down from generation to generation. In fact, that spark in a child that comes from books became the motivation for the creation of my organization, First Book, a national literacy program with a simple mission: to provide new books to the most disadvantaged children. At present, First Book has been at work in hundreds of communities for over a decade. Every year children in need receive millions of books through our organization and millions more are provided through dedicated literacy institutions across the United States and around the world. In addition, groups of people dedicate themselves tirelessly to working with children to share reading and stories in every imaginable setting from schools to the streets. Of course, this Herculean effort serves many important goals. Literacy translates to productivity and employability in life and many other valid and even essential elements. But at the heart of this movement are people who love stories, love to read, and want desperately to ensure that no one misses the wonderful possibilities that reading provides.

When thinking about the importance of books, there is an overwhelming urge to cite the literary devotion of great minds. Some have written of the magnitude of the importance of literature. Amy Lowell, an American poet, captured the concept when she said, "Books are more than books. They are the life, the very heart and core of ages past, the reason why men lived and worked and died, the essence and quintessence of their lives." Others have spoken of their personal obsession with books, as in Thomas Jefferson's simple statement: "I live for books." But more compelling, perhaps, is the almost instinctive excitement in children for books and stories.

Throughout my years at First Book, I have heard truly extraordinary stories about the power of books in the lives of children. In one case, a homeless child, who had been bounced from one location to another, later resurfaced— and the only possession that he had fought to keep was the book he was given as part of a First Book distribution months earlier. More recently, I met a child who, upon receiving the book he wanted, flashed a big smile and said, "This is my big chance!" These snapshots reveal the true power of books and stories to give hope and change lives.

As these children grow up and continue to develop their love of reading, they will owe a profound debt to those volunteers who reached out to them—a debt that they may repay by reaching out to spark the next generation of readers. But there is a greater debt owed by all of us— a debt to the storytellers, the authors, who have bound us together, inspired our leaders, fueled our civilizations, and helped us put our children to sleep with their heads full of images and ideas.

WHO WROTE THAT? is a series of books dedicated to introducing us to a few of these incredible individuals. While we have almost always honored stories, we have not uniformly honored storytellers. In fact, some of the most important authors have toiled in complete obscurity throughout their lives or have been openly persecuted for the uncomfortable truths that they have laid before us. When confronted with the magnitude of their written work or perhaps the daily grind of our own, we can forget that writers are people. They struggle through the same daily indignities and dental appointments, and they experience the intense joy and bottomless despair that many of us do. Yet somehow they rise above it all to deliver a powerful thread that connects us all. It is a rare honor to have the opportunity that these books provide to share the lives of these extraordinary people. Enjoy.

Author Anthony Horowitz has become famous for creating his teen spy book hero, Alex Rider. Shown here, at the launch of his new Alex Rider book, Ark Angel, in April 2005, Anthony (left) poses with actors playing Alex Rider (right) and one of the foes from Ark Angel (hanging), who is trying to steal a copy of the book from Foyles bookstore. Published in 2005, Ark Angel is Anthony's sixth book featuring Alex Rider.

1

Should I Keep Going?

ACCORDING TO ONE of Britain's leading newspapers, *The Guardian*:

> Anthony Horowitz is the master of bionic pimple cream (the ultimate adolescent accessory); exploding bubblegum (Bubble '07); a flame throwing palm organizer (Napalm organizer); and a talking "Get Well Soon" card that goes up in smoke after delivering its message. He is fiction's gadget king.
>
> But greater than any of his gadgets is Alex Rider, a reluctant teenage spy. Alex is a lonely, ordinary teenager from a comprehensive school [the English term for a state-run public school], with a

rucksack [backpack] full of homework. But homework ("To hell with it," he thought, "Irregular verbs could wait.") is on hold while Alex saves the world. *Stormbreaker*, *Point Blanc*, *Skeleton Key*, *Eagle Strike*, *Scorpia*—the Alex Rider series— has turned its author into a celebrity.[1]

In this, Anthony Horowitz is a rarity. Very few writers ever become celebrities. Most writers work their entire lives without being well known to anyone but family, friends, and, hopefully, a small circle of fans. For many years, it looked like Anthony would be no exception. He had been writing one children's book a year for over 20 years in relative obscurity before finally striking it big in the year 2000 with *Stormbreaker*—the first book in the highly successful Alex Rider series. Before *Stormbreaker* though, Anthony had found great success as a television writer. He was the creator and writer of the British television series *Murder in Mind*, *Midsomer Murders*, and *Foyle's War*. He also worked on *Poirot* for three seasons. This television work, in addition to his wife Jill's thriving career, allowed them to raise their two sons, Nicholas and Cassian, in comfort. But his children's books were another matter entirely.

Anthony had tried his hand at writing many genres— different types of books. He had written horror books: *Horowitz Horror* and *More Horowitz Horror* as well as the Power of Five series. He had written a historical novel set in the time of Shakespeare: *The Devil and His Boy*. He had written a series of tough guy detective stories featuring the Diamond Brothers, Nick and Tim. He had written a comic horror book based on his own grandmother, *Granny*. He had even written two books—*Groosham Grange* and *Return to Groosham Grange*—which feature a boy who goes to a magical school for witchcraft, 10 years before J.K. Rowling's first book about Harry Potter appeared on bookstore shelves. While some of his titles had respectable sales, none of them were what could be called highly successful by today's standards. But it is important to remember that very few children's titles ever sold in large numbers prior to the worldwide success of the Harry Potter series. It was the rare writer who was able to support himself (or herself) solely from writing children's books. Fortunately for Anthony, his extraordinary success as a television writer became his actual paying career, his bread and butter. Writing books for children was what he *wanted* to do. It was his labor of love. But should he continue to do it if people were not going to buy his books? One ex-publisher actually told him that he "might as well stop"[2] writing children's books. Anthony himself began to wonder whether he should continue. Maybe all the thought and effort that went into writing the books was not worth it. Why write them if nobody was going to read them?

Little did he know that an earthquake was about to hit the world of children's publishing. The year 1997 saw the British publication of the first Harry Potter title, *Harry Potter and the Sorcerer's Stone*. The huge sales for this, as well as for the ensuing Harry Potter titles, helped spark a renewed interest and sales in all children's literature. Publishers were on the lookout for the "next Harry." They were looking for a

Did you know...

Did you know that the latest title in the Harry Potter series, *Harry Potter and the Half Blood Prince*, sold 11,000,000 copies in its first two months of release in the United States? The total sales for the series worldwide exceeds 250,000,000 books!

character that could become as profitable for them as Harry was for his publisher, Bloomsbury Publishing Place.

It was around this time that Anthony began looking for an idea for his next book. As a writer he found that he often looked back on his own childhood. Not just at what actually happened, not just at his "real life," but his dream life as well. He guessed that if he had fantasized about something in particular, it was likely others did as well, and if this was the case, he thought that children would enjoy seeing *their* fantasies come to life on the page. Anthony said:

> When I was 8, 9, 10, 11, 12, and 13, the James Bond films were coming out for the first time. So . . . every year at Christmas I would go to see the new James Bond film. It was a big, big event in my life. First, there was *Dr. No*, then *From Russia with Love*, and *Goldfinger*. All of those films were made in the 1960s. I loved the James Bond books by Ian Fleming. I still think the books are really good, people have forgotten how good they are and how much better than the films. So Bond was a big, big, influence on me.
>
> And then I hated school. I was very miserable there and I was a rotten student: I was bottom [of my class] in everything. So I would dream that instead of being stuck in that dreadful school and being bullied and tormented by the teachers, that I was a spy. Thirty years later I remembered the dream and wrote a book about a teenage spy.[3]

So it was Anthony's unhappy childhood and his need to escape through fantasy that helped lead him to writing the novel *Stormbreaker* and creating the character of Alex Rider.

Stormbreaker was the breakthrough that Anthony had been waiting for. The book was a huge success, and Alex Rider became a favorite character for millions of young readers. In fact, *Stormbreaker* was the novel that, according

Growing up, Anthony Horowitz loved reading author Ian Fleming's James Bond series of books and watching the James Bond spy thriller films, which were based on Fleming's novels. Actor Sean Connery, the original Bond, is seen here on the set of Goldfinger *with one of Bond's cars, a 1964 Aston Martin DB5.*

to the *Ultimate Book Guide*, children want to see filmed more than any other. (Filming finally began in July of 2005, with Anthony himself writing the screenplay.) And the series itself, as one critic put it, "reads like a bored schoolboy's fantasy, only a thousand times slicker and more exciting."[4]

But, if Alex represents EVERY bored schoolboy's fantasy, why was Anthony the only writer able to put it onto paper? What, exactly, was Anthony's childhood like? How did Anthony Horowitz become one of the world's most successful children's book authors? How did a rich, pampered, fat, unhappy little boy come to create one of the coolest characters in contemporary children's literature?

Anthony Horowitz grew up in a family that had many privileges. He lived with his siblings and parents in a mansion in Stanmore, Middlesex, England. A housing development of 16 houses now stands where his family estate once stood. Stanmore in Middlesex, as shown above, now has more developments than mansions.

2

A Childhood Unlike Any Other

IT MAY BE TRUE that Anthony Horowitz grew up in a life that many Americans would view as one of privilege and luxury. It was certainly a life well-protected from the traumas and difficulties of growing up poor. But, as Anthony once pointed out, it is often this very suffering and unhappiness that helps to make a writer into a writer. He said:

> A little suffering never hurt a writing career. Think of Roald Dahl (author of *Charlie and the Chocolate Factory*) and the horrors of his childhood as described in his book *Boy*. Enid Blyton [the author

of *The Famous Five, and Noddy*], was supposedly influenced by (and never quite recovered from), the abrupt departure of her father when she was twelve. A large part of James Barrie's work [the author of *Peter Pan*], the boys who wouldn't grow up, was inspired by the death of his 13-year old brother, David. It could have been argued that Charles Dickens [noted 19th century British author], might never have written with such urgency and immediacy (and certainly he never would have met a man called Fagin [the villain in Dickens's novel *Oliver Twist*]), if he hadn't been condemned to a spell of abject poverty and an apprenticeship in a bottling factory in the Hungerford Steps.

My own childhood was, regrettably, devoid of any such luck. Quite the opposite: I was brought up by wealthy and loving parents in a large house in Stanmore, north London. I was privately educated. Nothing terrible ever happened. Other writers have had to overcome adversity; I sometimes feel I've had to overcome advantage.[5]

It is, however, equally true that a life of privilege is not enough to guarantee childhood happiness. And even though in the above quote Anthony attempts to downplay his own childhood unhappiness, in other interviews, it is another story. He has said:

I'm still dealing with the baggage of those unhappy years. I think a lot of my life has been a reaction to what I went through as a boy. I'd even say it's something that has a resonance for me every single day, even though I'd say I love my life and my multiple careers—today.[6]

Anthony Horowitz was born April 5, 1955, in Stanmore, Middlesex, England. His parents were Mark and Joyce Horowitz. His father was a solicitor. (In Britain, the positions known as attorneys or lawyers in the United States are known as solicitors and barristers. Solicitors generally give legal advice and do not appear in court, while barristers represent people in the courts of law.) More than that, he was also, as Anthony described him, "very broadly a business man."[7]

Mark Horowitz was also a very secretive man, so exactly what kind of business he was in was always unclear. Anthony was never certain as to what his father did with his time. He said:

> At one time he [Mark] was involved in something called Triumph Investment Bank but it went bust pretty spectacularly and he lost all his money. He had a circle of business partners who were all shady characters. Not crooks (I think), but on the fringes.[8]

Even when Anthony was a teenager, he was unsure of his father's business dealings. He said:

> All I know is that when I was 18 years old and had a motorbike and I rode across London carrying bearer bonds [bearer bonds are payable to WHOEVER holds the bonds themselves], worth a quarter of a million pounds [valued at over $500,000 at the 1973 exchange rate], that my father wanted me to pay to someone in an office. To this day I have no idea who the people were who received this money or how my father got the money in the first place or why I was carrying it.
>
> He was a solicitor by and large, but inhabited a world as mysterious as the ones I create, of codes and strange meetings and money on motorbikes. And when he died, when I was 22, he left behind books filled with codenames and notes and strange things.[9]

Anthony's childhood home was called White Friars. At this time, it was a large estate. The house is no longer there; in its place now stands 16 five-bedroom houses! Anthony remembers that it required many servants to run an estate of that size. There was Phyllis and Mary, two sisters who worked as housemaid and cook, respectively. There was Mr. Lampy the gardener (he appears in Anthony's novel *Granny*). There was an undergardener (assistant to the gardener) who was deaf. Mr. Smith was the handyman. Mrs. Smith helped in the house. Bob was the chauffeur.

Despite all the servants, and although he had both a brother and a sister, Anthony was often lonely. His father, Mark Horowitz, was away on business more often than not, and when he was home, he was cold and distant. In fact, he was so secretive that Anthony has few childhood memories of him. Although never cruel or unkind, Mark ran his household in what could be called a Victorian manner. This means that he, as the father, was the undisputed head of the household, and he felt it proper that he run his home with a strong hand. In addition, like most Victorian fathers, Mark did not often show his children a great deal of affection.

Dinnertime, for example, was an ordeal for young Anthony. After being summoned to the table by the sound of a loud gong, he and his older brother and younger sister were required to "sing for their supper." This means that they were required to provide intelligent and witty conversation. As Anthony later remembered:

Auberon Waugh [a well known British writer, son of legendary

Did you know...

Did you know that in England, public schools are called comprehensive schools?

British author Evelyn Waugh] was apparently allowed into his father's presence by the nanny for a brief period each week. Evelyn Waugh always made it clear that his work was his priority; my equivalent of that was tension at the dinner table. If I were insufficiently entertaining, I'd be summarily dismissed.[10]

Anthony was not dismissed from too many dinners though. As a child, he was overweight. He said, "Family meals had calories running into the thousands . . . I was an astoundingly large, round child . . ."[11] As he recalled, years later:

A typical meal was a starter, smoked salmon shall we say, followed by a main course, which might be some kind of meat with three vegetables. Then there would be a large pudding [A traditional English dessert, usually much heavier and more elaborate than, let's say, a simple American chocolate pudding]. There were just too many calories, the entire family collapsed asleep after Sunday lunch.[12]

There was of course more to his father than the distant dinnertime figure. Anthony was raised Jewish and Mark sent him to a Jewish Sunday school. Anthony said, "but 'I hate the Jews' was a favorite saying of his. He was joking."[13]

Mark was also a highly cultured man who loved opera, literature, and classical music. The Victorian novelists Anthony Trollope and William Makepeace Thackeray were his favorite authors and Anthony inherited Mark's library of 500 "serious" books. Oddly enough, despite his love of literature, Mark sneered at Anthony's desire to be a writer. Indeed, when Anthony was 16 or 17, Mark snuck into his son's bedroom and read a manuscript Anthony was working on and made jokes about it. He even made fun of it in front of the entire family! As Anthony describes his father, Mark was "a strange mix in a way. Jewish businessman vs. cultured + intelligent."[14]

Although his father was a rather scary and unapproachable figure, Anthony adored his mother and was very close to her. Joyce Horowitz was a socialite who went to parties, played bridge, and traveled. (Both of his parents are parodied in three of Anthony's books: *Granny*, *Groosham Grange*, and *Return to Groosham Grange*.) She loved gin and tonics and gambling at slot machines, but she and Anthony shared numerous happy times together, many of which were at bedtime, when Joyce would read her son horror stories. Anthony said:

> One of my earliest memories is of my mother coming to tuck me in bed and reading me horror stories, which were retellings of films that she had seen, such as *Dracula*, *Frankenstein*, *The Invisible Man*, and my favorite *The Fly* with Vincent Price. I have always loved horror. When I was thirteen, I asked my mother to buy me a human skull, which she did. I still have it to this day.[15]

Anthony's love of horror undoubtedly began with these late night storytelling sessions.

Of course, after the age of 8, Anthony lived away from home and saw very little of his parents. As was typical of a young man of his class, growing up in that time, Anthony was sent to live and learn at a boarding school. While he enjoyed being away from home, the school itself, named Orley Farm School, was a nightmare for him.

Unhappy and overweight, Anthony had a terrible time fitting in. The school was a very old-fashioned, Dickensian type of school; complete with a headmaster who literally flogged (whipped) his students. "Once," Anthony remembered, "the headmaster told me to stand up in assembly and in front of the whole school said, 'This boy is so stupid he will not be coming to the Christmas party tomorrow.' I have never fully recovered."[16] (Can you imagine what that must have felt like?)

But, and this is important, while Anthony was miserable at Orley Farm School, it is there that he first began writing. He said:

> At school in the sixties, I found an escape telling stories; elaborate fantasies involving two boys, Jimmy and Edward, who were always on the run. (Jimmy Edwards was a famous actor in English children's films back then.) From this beginning I can draw a straight line to what I write now. Fast-paced, action, adventure and jokes. Serious, only occasionally. Most of the time I just want to have fun.[17]

Telling stories allowed Anthony to forget his own unhappiness and create new, better, more exciting worlds to live in. He said:

> The impetus to tell stories grew out of my childhood. I was doing it when I was eleven years old, inventing stories and creating, partly to get away from the reality of what I was and where I was. I think that is the energy behind my books: the endless search for new escapades and surprises.[18]

So while Anthony may have had an unhappy childhood, in some ways he was very lucky. For many people, they are well into early adulthood before they settle in on a career, but not Anthony. The pleasure he had in telling stories to escape his own unhappiness convinced him early on that being a writer was what he wanted to do. Anthony later recalled just how his school experience helped him to become a writer:

I knew without a doubt that I would be a writer when I was eight years old. This was partly due to the fact that I was no good at anything else (still true today). I was sent to a really horrible boarding school in North London. It was an all boy's school. The headmaster was allowed to beat you and he often did. After lights out, I used to tell the other boys stories as a way of escape. I also discovered reading. The library was the only place in the school where I was happy. I wrote a play when I was ten. It was called "The Thing That Never Happened" and it was all about Guy Fawkes [Guy Fawkes was an Englishman who was executed for his part in a plot to blow up the Houses of Parliament and kill King James I in the year 1605.] I suppose I've been writing ever since.[19]

Anthony was, in effect, "saved by his own imagination."[20]

In 1968, Anthony moved from Orley Farm School to Rugby School. Here, for perhaps the first time in his life, Anthony was completely happy. Instead of a cruel headmaster, Rugby School was run by a headmaster who treated the students with kindness and respect. It was here, as Anthony reached adolescence that he began to gain confidence and make friends. And, it was here that Anthony was introduced to books by the writers who became the loves of his literary life.

Most people are fortunate to have at least one teacher who really makes a difference in their lives. At Rugby School, Anthony had three: Mr. Alden, Mr. Helliwell, and Mr. Brown. These three English teachers introduced Anthony to classics written by some of the greatest writers in the English language: William Shakespeare, Jane Austen, and, perhaps most importantly to Anthony, Charles Dickens.

Charles Dickens (1812–1870) was a writer who wrote

Charles Dickens, shown here, wrote many classics, including Anthony Horowitz's favorite novel, Great Expectations. *Anthony loves the depth and fast pace of Dickens's writing, and this introduction to great fiction was just the start Anthony needed to begin his own writing career.*

what some consider among the greatest novels ever written. In such books as *Oliver Twist*, *David Copperfield*, and *Bleak House*, Dickens told exciting stories made memorable with a vivid panorama of colorful and interesting characters. Of all of Dickens works (he wrote 14 novels and numerous shorter works), Anthony responded most strongly to one of Dicken's greatest books, *Great Expectations*.

Great Expectations was first published in book form in 1862. (Victorian novels like *Great Expectations* were often first published in monthly magazines, a few chapters at a time. This kept readers buying the magazines to find out what was going to happen next. In this way, it was very much like television soap operas, which leave audiences with a "cliffhanger" to get them to watch the next episode.) *Great Expectations* tells of the adventures of a young orphan named Philip Pirrip, better known as "Pip." The book was, and still remains, Anthony's favorite novel. Of the book he says:

> *Great Expectations* is my favorite novel, although [that] changes from time to time. Charles Dickens is just the great writer I've ever come across. His scope, his characters, his ability to mix serious social content with comedy and thrills with a very strong, fast paced Victorian plot. *Great Expectations* has his most memorable characters (like Miss Havisham). It has the wonderful cemetery scene at the beginning with Magwitch and I think it has the most ambiguous and interesting central character in Pip.[21]

In 1973, Anthony graduated from Rugby School. He had enjoyed his time there. The supportive atmosphere, so different from Orley Farm, had given him greater confidence in himself. And, the professors there had introduced him to writing that would have the greatest influence on his own.

There would be a few bumps along his road to success though. Bumps and surprises that Anthony could have never imagined.

Although Anthony Horowitz loved his time spent at Rugby School, shown above, after graduation Anthony decided to delay his university studies for a year and discover what life was like outside of England's private schools. Anthony traveled from Australia, to Singapore, before returning home.

Changes

AFTER LEAVING RUGBY SCHOOL, instead of going directly to college at the University of York, Anthony decided to take a full year break. He thought that after so much time in private schools, he needed to see something of the real world. And so he did.

For nine months, Anthony lived in Australia, working as a "jackaroo," sort of an Australian cowboy. And then, instead of flying home from Australia, he took an additional three months traveling by himself over land from Singapore to England!

Although Anthony left the University of York in 1977 with a

Bachelor of Arts degree, he did not take his time in college all that seriously. For him it was a time of "very little work, but a lot of drama, a lot of writing plays, [and] a lot of having fun."[22]

In 1977, when Anthony was just 22 years old, his father died of a heart attack. In addition to this loss, there was an additional shock. His family was now penniless, due to a chain of events stranger than any fiction. Shortly before his death, Mark Horowitz faced the possibility of bankruptcy. In an attempt to hide his money from his debtors, he withdrew all the family's money from their usual Zurich, Switzerland, bank accounts and deposited it in another account, in another bank, using a false name. Unfortunately, he had told no one how the money could be found.

Anthony's mother did find a small black leather notebook that Mark had filled with code names and strange markings that he had apparently used to represent the bank accounts. She took the notebook to Zurich, but was unable to find the accounts. Joyce kept trying to find the money for the rest of her life, but the family money was lost forever. The Horowitz family's lives would never be the same.

By this time, of course, Anthony was living on his own, but it was different for his mother, who had been used to a life of money and comfort. Anthony fondly recalled:

> She reinvented herself completely when she woke up to find that every penny she owned had disappeared in the debts my father had left when he died. She really had nothing. So from being a wealthy socialite she had to go back to work as a company secretary, which she did with a great deal of cheerfulness.[23]

Interestingly enough, according to Anthony, the last 10 years of her life were among Joyce's happiest.

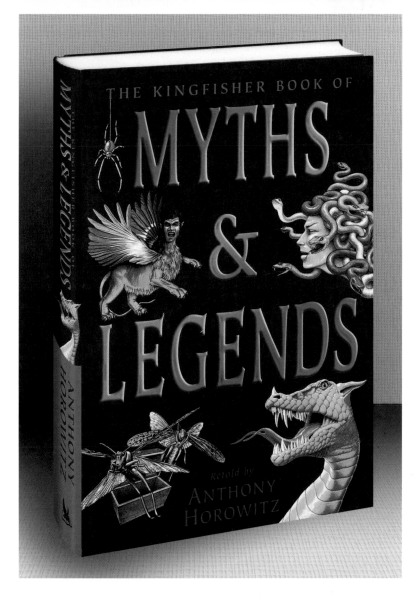

After working on The Kingfisher Book of Myths and Legends *(1985), which includes a myth about Robin Hood, Anthony Horowitz was inspired to submit a script for the television show* Robin of Sherwood *that was being filmed at the time. As a result of all the research that Anthony had done for* The Kingfisher Book of Myths and Legends, *his television script was richly detailed and the producers loved it!*

The loss of one's father is always difficult, no matter how one felt about him when he was alive. So how did Anthony feel about his loss? How does a son look back on a man like Mark Horowitz? How, ultimately, does a father contribute to what the son becomes? As Anthony said in 2004, more than 25 years after his father's death:

> Having a high-achieving father hardly provided a role model for me, unless your role model happens to be a multi-millionaire whose money vanishes into various Swiss accounts, never to be seen again, who dies of heart attack at the age of 55. Well, I suppose one legacy might be that in many ways I don't really trust that anything in life will continue as one might wish it to.[24]

This is, of course, a perfectly understandable response. Going from a life of money to a life without money, who would not feel that way? That nothing in life is forever. But Anthony had to move forward and get on with his life. He knew, as he had always known, that he wanted to be a writer. He also knew, that he needed to earn a living in the meantime, so he began working as a copywriter for various advertising agencies, finally taking a position at the advertising firm of McCann Erickson.

As a copywriter, it was Anthony's job to write the words used in print and radio advertisements. He even received awards for his work in radio! Anthony considered advertising, just as a way to pay the bills, but working at McCann Erickson did one have one positive benefit. It was there that he met his future wife, Jill Green.

Their relationship did not begin smoothly. She was an account manager at the agency, and Anthony worked for her. According to *The Guardian* "it was mutual hatred at first sight, and yet Anthony knew from the start, mid-argument, that they must marry."[25]

The animosity faded though after their first "date." Jill had to travel to a local amusement park, Alton Towers, for business. Anthony, who loves amusement parks, persuaded Jill to bring him along. They had a great time that afternoon on all the rides. Then, on the way home, the radio aired a discussion of a radio play that Anthony had written. And so began their relationship.

But although his relationship with Jill was progressing nicely, Anthony knew he did not want to work at McCann Erickson much longer. He wanted to be a writer. And one day he was. He said:

> It was never my intention to be a children's book author. I wasn't a parent. I wasn't married. One wet afternoon at the advertising agency. And it was wet, I remember it raining. I was bored, and I didn't know what to do with myself. And without any planning or structuring or thinking, I just wrote the opening page of a children's book. I just remember writing "Frederick K. Bauer was the most unpleasant boy in the world" or something to that effect . . . And I finished it,

Did you know...

Did you know that Anthony Horowitz wrote *The Kingfisher Book of Myths and Legends* for a straight fee, rather than for royalties per copy sold? Unfortunately for Anthony, the book was a huge success and has never been out of print; Anthony lost out on making a lot of money!

and sometime later met someone at a party who wanted to be an agent who brought it to a man named Desmond Elliot who published it.[26]

That book, no longer in print, was followed by *Misha, the Magician and the Mysterious Amulet.* That early work too, is no longer in print, much to Anthony's relief. "*Amulet* is one I never talk about. There were some good things, but it was misguided. It is a bad book. Thank God it's out of print."[27]

Shortly after this, Anthony came down with glandular fever, and was at home longer than a month recuperating. While resting, he began work on *The Kingfisher Book of Myths and Legends.* Robin Hood is one of the characters in the book, and Anthony did a lot of research about him. At the same time, the television series *Robin of Sherwood* had begun filming. Anthony's agent suggested he send in an idea for story. The idea he sent was so detailed and on target, since he had just done the research on Robin Hood, that the producers asked him to turn it into a screenplay. One screenplay led to a second, then a third. And so Anthony's career as a television writer was born.

But while his television writing career was beginning to take off, the same was not true of his children's books. In 1983, the first book in The Power of Five series, *The Devil's Doorbell*, was published. This book concerned the struggles of orphan Martin Hopkins against supernatural forces of evil. Other titles followed: *The Night of the Scorpion* (1984), *The Silver Citadel* (1986), and *Day of the Dragon* (1989). The series received good reviews.

Anne Connor called *The Devil's Doorbell* "a satisfyingly scary book,"[28] in the *School Library Journal.* The books had moderate sales, but are now out of print. (They will, however, make a return appearance later in Anthony's career.) Fantasy books were not selling for Anthony. He knew he would have to try something else.

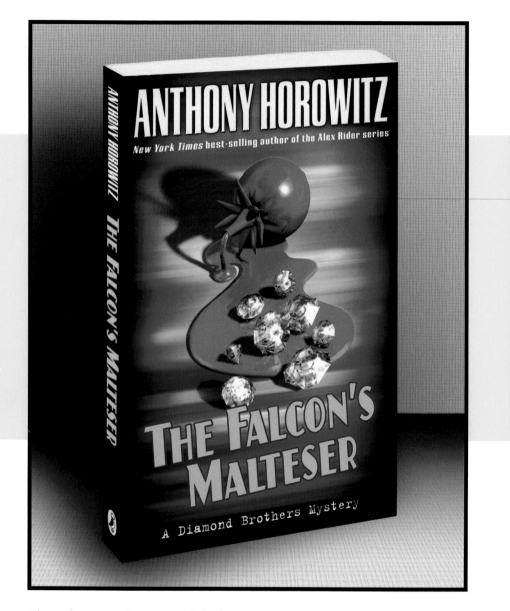

The Falcon's Malteser, *published in 1986, was the first in Anthony Horowitz's series of humorous detective stories featuring the Diamond Brothers, Nick and Tim. A fan of old movies, Anthony's writing was inspired by many of the hard-boiled detective films of the 1930s, '40s, and '50s.*

4

Starting Over

THE FIRST DIAMOND Brothers book, *The Falcon's Malteser*, was originally published in England in 1986. (It was finally published in the United States in 2004. The publishers hoped to take advantage of the popularity of the Alex Rider series.) As in all of his books, the hero in *The Falcon's Malteser* is a reflection, of sorts, of Anthony. He said:

> . . . all my child heroes have been the exact opposite of me. There is Nick Diamond, the 13-year-old detective who has now appeared in six books. His parents have emigrated to Australia without taking him. He lives in a grubby flat in Camden with his inept older

brother, cold beans for breakfast, and low-life thugs on every street corner.[29]

The book itself, a humorous detective story, is also a take-off on an old classic novel and movie, *The Maltese Falcon*. Anthony remembered, "The inspiration for these was simply an odd thought I had one day, which was to take my favorite film, *The Maltese Falcon*, and suddenly [I] began to think about *The Falcon's Malteser* and then I began to think about having a Sam Space character who was fourteen."[30]

In the original story, private detective Sam Spade is hired by a colorful assortment of crooks to find a valuable statue of a bird once owned by the Knights of Malta: the Maltese Falcon. In his affectionate satire, Anthony takes a slightly different spin on the story. As *Booklist* described it in its 2004 review:

> Thirteen-year-old Nick is the younger (and brighter) half of the Diamond Brothers, the world's worst detective agency. Dwarf Johnny Naples becomes their client entrusting the two with a mysterious package (a box of Malteser chocolates) just before he is killed, leaving Tim Diamond, literally, holding the gun. With Tim in jail, Nick is forced to solve the case—hopefully before someone murders him too . . . Horowitz's classic cast of quirky villains—including The Fat Man, Gott and Himmel [a pair of villains whose names are a pun on a German phrase meaning God in heaven], Beatrice Van Valkenberg, and the Professor—and non stop action, and clever deadpan humor ensure that the novel will be a popular choice.[31]

The book was popular in England on its original publication. So popular in fact, that it inspired five additional books, a movie, and a television series. As much as Anthony loved writing the books, the movie and television series were another matter. He said:

The movie . . . was a great disappointment. It had a very good cast, but perhaps not enough money behind it and maybe the wrong director and even a script that could have been better [Anthony wrote the screenplay], and certainly a leading child who very much let the side down. His name was Colin Dale. The television series (*The Diamond Brothers*, 1991) was also disappointing. I directed it myself. I wasn't really prepared for that. I had no training, no real idea of what I was doing. It was a little bit of a nightmare . . .[32]

In writing the books though, Anthony was in complete control. And control, having the final say on your work, is essential to a writer or to any artist for that matter. So although Anthony at this stage of his career was earning the majority of his living by writing for television, he relished the control that writing books could give him. Anthony discussed this in his interview with *Write Away!*:

Television is collaboration. When you write for television you are not necessarily writing what will appear on the screen because the director may not direct the actors to say the lines the way you wanted them to be spoken; the clothes person may dress the characters in a different way to what you saw; the props master may buy different sorts of guns or pens to what you had imagined; and the set dresser may decide not to build the set the way you thought because it's too expensive to go to Murmansk. So it all changes and in the end it comes out as a bit of your work. But with a book, every single word I write is the word you'll read. Nobody else does anything— an editor does a bit of work and advises but it's my writing and my writing alone. So, that is the single biggest difference: A book is my work and television is a collaboration.[33]

And with control, Anthony was able to indulge his love of non-stop action, his love of old movies (the movie *North by*

Northwest became *South by South East*, *The Third Man* became *The Blurred Man*, *The French Connection* became *The French Confection*), and perhaps most interestingly in these books, his sense of humor.

Anthony likes absurd humor told with a perfectly straight face, he loves wordplay and puns, and all of these aspects of Anthony are on full display in the Diamond Brothers series. (The Diamond Brothers books are all told in the first person, with Nick as the narrator.) For example, this description of Tim as told by his younger brother Nick:

> Dark-haired and blue-eyed, Herbert [he calls himself "Tim"] was quite handsome—at least from the opposite side of the street on a foggy day. But what God had given him in looks, He had taken away in brains. There might have been worse private detectives than Tim Diamond. But somehow I doubt it.
>
> I'll give you an example. His first job was to find some rich lady's pedigree Siamese cat. He managed to run it over on the way to see her. The second job was a divorce case—which you might think is run-of-the-mill until I tell you that the clients were perfectly happily married until he came along.
>
> There hadn't been a third case. (*Falcon's Malteser* 10)

Tim is, in fact, stupid:

Did you know...

Did you know that despite Anthony Horowitz's love of most old movies, his least favorite movie is *The Wizard of Oz*? It is true! He thinks the Munchkins are boring, the witches are not wicked enough, and the ending is a complete copout!

"He comes to us. He's in the street and he happens to see your name on the door. You're a private detective. That's perfect. And maybe your name rings a bell."

"No, Nick," Herbert interrupted. "It's the little button by the door that rings the bell . . ." (*The Falcon's Malteser* 56–57)

Much of the humor of the books derives from this simple fact. And Tim seems to get even more stupid in each succeeding book. Without Nick's brains, Tim would not stand a chance:

"Who are you?" Tim asked.

"My name's Lovely."

"I'm sure it is," Tim agreed. "But what is it?" (*Three of Diamonds* 26)

Anthony's young readers love jokes like this. But Anthony is also eager to include jokes and references that young readers might not quite understand such as:

"I need a bath," I said.

She shook her head. "Of all the baths in all the towns in all the world, you have to walk into mine . . ." (*The Falcon's Malteser* 135)

And:

Powers paused and I was amazed to see a tear trickle down one of his pale, choirboy cheeks.

"Ya don't know my ma," he said. "She's as tough as old nails. She's a real killer. And her cooking! Nobody makes a moussaka like her—all hot and bubbling with the cheese melted on top. She sent me one here, back in February."

"The St. Valentine's Day moussaka?" I asked. (*Public Enemy Number Two* 62)

Anthony Horowitz's The Falcon's Malteser *was inspired by the 1941 classic film* The Maltese Falcon, *which stars Humphrey Bogart as the hard-nosed detective, Sam Spade. In the scene shown here, Spade talks with the widow of his late partner, Miles Archer, who is played by actress Gladys George.*

The first excerpt is a take-off on a line from the classic 1940's movie *Casablanca*, which stars Humphrey Bogart. Bogart also starred in the movie *The Maltese Falcon* in 1941. (The original line in *Casablanca* is, "Of all the gin joints in all the towns in all the world, she walks into mine," but the line is often misquoted in Englad as "Of all the *bars* in the world.") The second selection is a pun on the famous Chicago gangland murders of the 1920s known as The St. Valentine's Day Massacre. Anthony knows full well that most of his younger readers are not going to understand all of his references. (Although they may still enjoy the lines themselves.) So if they are not included for his typical readers, why are they there at all? Anthony explained:

A lot of the lines in my books, particularly in the Diamond Brothers, are written just to amuse myself, a nod to parents who might, I hope, read the books to their kids at night. I'm a great supporter of parents reading with kids and offer up lines and little inside jokes if you like. In fact, the books are full of jokes that nobody else in the world gets, but me. Film references, anagrams, secret codes, messages, they're all in there. Maybe one day, a hundred years from now, somebody will work them all out, but I very much doubt it.[34]

The Diamond Brothers series (*The Falcon's Malteser*, 1986; *Public Enemy Number Two*, 1987; *South by South East*, 1991; *The French Confection*, 2002; *I Know What You Did Last Wednesday*, 2002; and *The Blurred Man*, 2002 [the last three titles were published as one volume in the United States, *Three of Diamonds*, 2005]) brought Anthony to a new, slightly higher level of popularity.

He was also growing as a writer. In the Diamond Brothers, for the first time, he allowed elements of himself to enter his characters. As he put it, "Tim and Nick are both me. Nick is how I wish I had been as a kid; Tim is me as I was."[35] In his next books, Anthony truly began to explore and use his childhood in his writing. And with that, he reached a turning point, both in his career, and as a writer.

Anthony Horowitz did not enjoy his time at Orley Farm School (pictured here). However, as a writer he found he was able to draw upon his experiences at the school and use them to create the fictional world of Groosham Grange, published in 1988.

5

Finding His Voice

IN 1988, ANTHONY PUBLISHED *Groosham Grange*. This book, written 13 years before J.K. Rowling's series on Harry Potter, follows the adventures of David Eliot in his first year at Groosham Grange, an academy of witchcraft.

Like Harry, David has an unhappy home life. Like Harry, David is mysteriously summoned to attend Groosham Grange. Like Harry, he has two friends, Jill and Jeffrey. But, unlike Harry, David does not want to be at Groosham Grange. David spends most of the book resisting his teachers and trying to escape. It is only at the end of the book that David learns to embrace who he is (the seventh son of the seventh son and so blessed with magical powers) and to appreciate and use those powers.

What is important about *Groosham Grange* (and its sequel *Return to Groosham Grange*), in terms of Anthony and his development as a writer, is not so much the fantasy element of the book, but his use of humor and of his experiences with his own parents and schooling.

When we first meet David, he gives his report card from his old school (this is before he is summoned to Groosham Grange) to his parents. Note Anthony's use of humor and wordplay:

> "Eliot has not made progress," the math teacher had written. "He can't divide or multiply and will, I fear, add up to very little."
>
> "Woodwork?" the carpentry teacher had written. "I wish he would work!"
>
> "If he stayed awake in class it would be a miracle," the religion teacher had complained.
>
> "Very poor form," the form master had concluded.
>
> "He'll never get ahead," the headmaster had agreed. (*Groosham Grange* 7–8)

David's parents (a satirical version of Anthony's own parents) are not pleased with David's report card.

> Mr. Eliot had read all these comments with growing anger. First his face had gone red. Then his fingers had gone white. The veins in his neck had gone blue and his tongue had gone black. Mrs. Eliot had been unsure whether to call a doctor or take a colour photograph, but in the end, and after several glasses of whiskey, he had calmed down.
>
> "When I was a boy," he moaned, "if my reports weren't first class, my father would lock me in a cupboard for a week without food. Once he chained me behind the car and drove

up the M1 and that was only because I came second equal in Latin."

"Where did we go wrong?" Mrs. Eliot sobbed, pulling at her mauve-tinted hair. "What will the neighbours say if they find out? They'll laugh at me! I'm ruined!"

"My father would have killed me if I'd had a report like this," Mr. Eliot continued. "He'd have tied me down to the railway line and waited for the 11.05 from Charing Cross . . ."

"We could always pretend we haven't got a son," Mrs. Eliot wailed. "We could say he's got a rare disease. We could say he fell off a cliff."

As you will have gathered from all of this, Mr. and Mrs. Eliot were not the best sort of parents you could hope to have. Edward Eliot was a small, fat, bald man with a bristling moustache and a wart on his neck. He was the head of a bank in the City of London. Eileen Eliot was about a foot taller than him, very thin with porcelain teeth and false eyelashes . . . (*Groosham Grange* 8–9)

By making fun of his parents, by exaggerating them to the point that they become laughable, Anthony was able to laugh at them himself. For example: "Mrs. Eliot in a bright pink dressing gown with matching hair curlers, hid behind the *Daily Mail* and slipped a little vodka into her cereal bowl. She liked a breakfast with schnapps, crackle and pop" (*Groosham Grange* 16).

He did the same thing with his experiences at school. As we know, Anthony hated Orley Farm School with a passion. Instead of drawing a darkly realistic portrayal of the school in *Groosham Grange*, through the power of his imagination Anthony turned it into a true school of horrors. The cruel headmaster at Orley Farm School is transformed into a headmaster who literally has two heads. The uncaring teachers and staff become an assistant headmaster who is a vampire, and a staff that includes ghosts, a werewolf, and a teacher who has lived forever. By blowing them all up to the point of absurdity, they become figures of fun, and lose part of their power to frighten.

A second volume, *Return to Groosham Grange*, followed *Groosham Grange*, published in 1991. In this sequel, David fights the efforts of a mysterious villain to take control of the "Unholy Grail" and by doing so, give him the power to destroy the school. On reading this book, the reader senses Anthony's pleasure in writing it. Particularly in the scenes where through the power of the "Unholy Grail" David's father is transformed into a warthog and his mother is sent to work in a rice paddy in China!

Although those two books remain favorites of Anthony's, sales fell short of Anthony's ambitious hopes. Nevertheless, the books have never been out of print for 15 years and have always been hugely popular in France. In the end, what was supposed to become a longer series ended with *Return to Groosham Grange*.

Fortunately for Anthony, in 1989—at the same time he was working on the books about David—Anthony was writing the screenplays for seven shows in the popular *Poirot* television series. These were based on the character Hercule Poirot created by the legendary British mystery writer Dame Agatha Christie. The shows were popular both in England and the United States, and Anthony wrote additional screenplays throughout the years, ultimately adapting three novels and nine short stories to the small screen. They were so successful, that Anthony nearly gave up the idea of writing children's books altogether. He said:

> I got fed up with the whole idea of writing children's books. My career, my TV career was bubbling along very very nicely. I'd done *Robin of Sherwood*. I'd done *The Adventures*

British actor David Suchet portrayed television's detective Hercule Poirot, in the show **Poirot,** *which was based on the Agatha Christie series. In 1989 Anthony Horowitz wrote seven of the scripts for the British show.*

of William Tell which was unspeakably awful, every script I wrote was rewritten massively by other people, so I don't think a single word of mine was ever really filmed. At the same time, they paid me so much money that I now had a little house, a little flat. I was also working on *Poirot* and other television shows that were always very mainstream TV shows. And I was doing these children's books, always waiting for them to be big, to be recognized, and I didn't think they ever were. I mean, they were doing OK; there were some nice reviews here and there, sales of maybe 10,000 a year, very unspectacular. It really was so frustrating, because, by this stage in my career, I always said to Jill that I'd be recognized as a children's writer. I knew that nobody was writing books like mine. But I just gave up altogether and said, "The hell with it," I'll just stick with television. Until Wendy Boase came and found me. She was from Walker Books and said "Look, we love your old books and we'll republish them, and at the same time let's start again and see what happens." So I did.[36]

Anthony's success as a television writer, and his new contract with Walker, gave him new freedom and confidence as a writer. His first book for his new publisher was *Granny*, his most revealing novel to date, about which he says, "*Granny* is my most personal novel. I decided to write it at her [my grandmother's] funeral, a very happy occasion . . . my brother, my sister and I danced on the old woman's grave and writing it was a pleasure, payback time for all the unhappiness she brought, not just to me, but to my parents."[37]

Usually, when someone says "I danced on her grave" they do not mean it literally. Like when someone says, "I could have danced all night," it is hyperbole, an exaggerated way of expressing a real feeling. However in this case it was not hyperbole. Anthony and his siblings *actually* danced on their grandmother's grave. What sort of woman's death would bring happiness to her own grandchildren? Anthony says:

It was her meanness. She was an incredibly mean woman. I think the worst thing you can do on this planet is to live here for 93 years and give pleasure to nobody. And that's what she managed to do. She had an argument with one of her children and didn't speak to him for twenty five years. She didn't meet his children, her own grandchildren, until they were adults. She was wealthy and comfortable and complained the whole time. Her whole life was only about how miserable *she* was. She was really evil. She was someone who could do so much and give so much and do nothing and give nothing. You're meant to believe that the grandmother is a good character. But you realize she's actually mean and nasty and doesn't particularly like you. She was a small evil person.[38]

Obviously, Esther Charatan, Anthony's grandmother on his mother's side, inspired deep feelings of dislike. Here is where being a writer can be an advantage. Other people might need to speak to a therapist, or a clergyman, or good friends in order to work through their feelings about such a person. Not Anthony. By writing about her, by being able to put his feelings about her on paper, he was able to work through his emotions. And by making the fictional "Granny" such a complete, over-the-top monster, he was able to place his real grandmother in a more human perspective.

And Granny is a true monster. When you read this initial description, you'll notice how it builds and builds until it is so exaggerated, that it becomes funny. This illustrates Anthony's technique: when you are able to laugh at something, it will no longer be quite as scary.

There was a time when Joe had liked his granny and had looked forward to her visits . . . But as he grew older, he had begun to notice things about his granny that he had not noticed before.

First there were the physical details: the terrible caves in her wrists where the skin seemed to sag underneath the veins, the blotchy patches on her legs, the whiskers on her upper lip and the really quite enormous mole on her chin. She had no dress sense whatsoever. She had, for example, worn the same coat for twenty-seven years and it had probably been second-hand when she bought it . . .

Then there were her table manners. Although it's a sad thing to say, Granny's table manners would have made a cannibal sick. She had a large mouth framed by some of the yellowest teeth in the world. These teeth were stumpy and irregular, slanting at odd angles, and actually wobbled in her gums when she laughed. But how hard they worked! Granny would eat at a fantastic rate, shoveling food in with a fork, lubricating it with a quick slurp of water and then swallowing it with a little sucking noise and a final hiccup. Sitting at the table, she would remind you of a cement mixer at a building site and watching her eat was both fascinating and repulsive at the same time.

Another aspect of her bad table manners was her tendency to steal the silver. After lunch with Granny, Mr. Warden would insist on a spoon count. Wolfgang and Irma would spend hours in the pantry checking off the pieces that remained against the pieces that had been laid and then writing down a long list of what would have to be replaced. When Granny left the house at half past four or whenever, her twenty-seven-year-old coat would be a lot bulgier then when she arrived, and as she leaned over to kiss Joe goodbye, he would hear the clinking in her pockets. On one occasion, Mrs. Warden embraced her mother too enthusiastically and actually impaled herself on a fruit knife. After that, Mr. Warden installed a metal detector in the front door which did at least help.

But nobody in the family ever mentioned this—either to each other or to anyone else . . . Nobody acted as if anything was wrong. (*Granny* 19–20)

Eventually, Joe finds Granny so physically repulsive that he can barely bring himself to kiss her.

Kissing Granny was not a pleasant experience. First there was the smell. Like many old ladies, she wore an expensive perfume that was very sweet and very musty and, if you got too close to it, made you feel a little sick. There were no labels on her perfume bottles but this one might have been called "Decomposing Sheep". Then there was her make-up. Sometime she put it on so thickly that you could have drawn a picture in it with your thumb-nail. Her lipstick was the worst bit. It was bright blood red and no matter how carefully Joe tried, he always came away with a glowing mirror-image of Granny's lips on his cheek. Nobody knew what make of lipstick used, but Mrs. Jinks could only get it off him with a Brillo pad.

But worst of all was her skin. As well as kissing her grandson, Granny insisted on his kissing her and her skin was as withery as a punctured balloon. No words could describe the feel of her skin against his lips, actually flapping slightly between the upper and the lower lip at the moment of kissing. One night Joe had woken up screaming. He had just had a nightmare in which he had kissed Granny too enthusiastically and had actually swallowed her whole. (*Granny* 27–28)

Even though Granny tries to pretend that she is really a sweet loving grandmother, it is just a mask she wears to hide her true feelings. Joe learns through the course of the book that Granny is not only ugly on the outside, but she is ugly on the inside as well. For example, Granny purposely gives Joe a Christmas present he is far too old for. One look at her face and Joe never feels the same about her again.

He heard his granny's voice and looked up. And that was when he finally knew. There was something in her face that he had never seen before and now that he had noticed it he would never be able to see her any other way again. It was like one of those optical illusions you sometimes find in cereal packets. You look at a picture one way but then you suddenly notice something different and you can never see it again the same way.

He was right.

She had done it on purpose.

She knew exactly what he wanted and she had gone out and deliberately chosen this baby toy to humiliate him in front of the entire family. Of course, his mother would try to explain that Granny meant well and that she hadn't understood what he wanted. He would be made to write a thank you letter and every lying word would hurt him. But at that moment, looking at her, he knew the truth. He could see it in the wicked glimmer in her eyes, in the half-turned corner of her mouth. And it was so strong, so horrible that he shivered.

She was *evil*. For reasons that he did not yet understand, Granny hated him and wanted to hurt him in any way she could. (*Granny* 32–33)

On another occasion, Granny invites Joe to tea. But when he arrives he finds that she is not serving anything that he would want to eat.

First, there were egg mayonnaise sandwiches, but the eggs had been left out so long that the yellows had taken on a greenish tint and they had so much salt in them that they made your eyes water. There was herring on a plate—raw and slippery and soused in some sort of particularly sharp vinegar. Granny's homemade cakes were dry and heavy, guaranteed to glue the top of your mouth to the bottom of your mouth with little taste in between. Even the biscuits were horrible: round, colourless things with neither chocolate nor cream but decorated with almond flakes and bits of desiccated cherry that got caught in your teeth.

But by far the worst item on the table was Granny's cream cheese special. Joe caught sight of it and felt his mouth water unpleasantly and his stomach shrivel as if trying to find somewhere to hide. Granny's cream cheese special consisted of just one thing: cream cheese. That was all it was: a big bowl of cream cheese—and he knew that he would be expected to eat it all.

She put the serviettes [napkins] down and picked up a green porcelain bowl, filled to the brim with thick cream cheese. Then she forked out a raw herring and laid it on the top. "That'll give it extra taste," she cackled. Finally she slid the whole thing towards him and as she did so Joe saw the trembling half-smile on her lips, the rattlesnake eyes that pinned him to his seat. Her long, knobbly fingers with their uneven, yellow nails were scratching at the tablecloth with sheer excitement. Her whole body was coiled up like a spring.

"Now, eat it all up, dear!" (*Granny* 39–41)

Then, through careful plotting, Granny manages to dispose of everybody in Joe's life who could protect him. For example, his nanny, Mrs. Jinks, is falsely accused of stealing a brooch from Granny and two of Mr. Warden's gold teeth. She then disappears after being attacked by police dogs after Granny surreptitiously sprinkles gravy mix on her coat.

And, since it is summer vacation, both the cook and the butler are gone, leaving the Warden's to cook and clean for themselves, something they are incapable of doing. In the following excerpt, Anthony uses exaggeration and humor to draw a picture of a family that cannot cope on their own:

"I'm going shopping this afternoon," she [Mrs. Warden] said. "I thought I'd go to the spring sales. The sofa in the living room needs some new springs. Then tea at the Ritz and I should be home in time for supper."

"Do you want me to make the supper?" Joe asked.

"I don't think so, darling!" Mrs. Warden giggled. "Leave that to me!"

But in fact she was so exhausted after her day's shopping that she quite forgot to cook. That evening, Mr. Warden and Joe sat at the table staring gloomily at three tins [cans] of pink salmon. Mrs. Warden was even gloomier. She couldn't find the tin opener.

On Tuesday the dishwasher broke down, much to the horror of Mrs. Warden, who hadn't washed a dish herself since 1963 (and then she had only rinsed it). The next day she went out and bought a hundred paper plates which were fine with the main courses and puddings but caused problems with the soup.

On Wednesday, Mr. Warden attempted to dry his shoes by placing them in the microwave. His feet were actually glowing as he took the tube [subway] to work and he caused a bomb scare at Charing Cross.

On Thursday, the toaster exploded when Mr. Warden tried to light it with a match.

On Friday it was the Hoover. Mrs. Warden only just escaped a terrible injury when she tried to use it to blow-dry her hair. (*Granny* 65–66)

At this point, *Granny*'s narrator expresses his feelings about the family's predicament:

You may think it pathetic that Mr. and Mrs. Warden were so incapable of looking after themselves but you'd be surprised how true this is of the very rich. They've been looked after by servants for so long that they don't know how to do anything for themselves. Ask the Queen what a Brillo pad is and she'd probably tell you it was a lovely place to live. (*Granny* 66)

Is the narrator in this book expressing Anthony's own point of view? Given what we know of Anthony's feelings about his family, it seems entirely possible.

Finally though, in desperation, Granny is moved into the Warden family's house, and Joe's parents escape to their flat in the south of France. Joe is now completely in Granny's power.

Late one night, while listening in on a card game between Granny and four of her friends, Joe learns the terrible truth about how these old grannies really feel about young people.

"How I hate children!" the vulture granny moaned.

"Me too!"

"I can't stand them."

"I detest them!"

"You know what I hate about them?" Granny Smith said. "I hate their perfect skin. It's all pink and shiny and smooth. I hate their hair, so thick and wavy. But most of all I hate their teeth." She gazed at her own on the table in front of her. "Do you know where children keep their teeth? In their mouths! It isn't fair."

"I hate children because they're so healthy," Granny Anne went on. "They're always shouting and playing and having fun and running about. I haven't run anywhere since 1958 and that was only for a bus."

"I hate them because of everything they've got," Granny Adams muttered. "We never had computers and pop music and T-shirts and mountain bikes. But they have. I fought in two world wars but nobody ever gave me a skateboard. Oh no!"

"Children smell," Granny Lee announced. "They're too small and they make too much noise. Why can't they be more like us?"

"Yes. With arthritis!"

"And swollen knees."

"Hard of hearing!"

"What?"

"And wrinkly."

"Horrid! Horrid! Horrid! Horrid! Horrid!" (*Granny* 82–84)

But if grannies hate children, they all have their own ways of getting revenge. They poke them. They pat them on their heads. Give them wet messy kisses. Give them presents that they know they will hate like talcum powder, or a book mark. They buy them ugly clothing that they know they'll have to wear. According to *Granny*, all the things people think that grannies do because they are old and do not know any better, they are really doing on purpose!

As in Roald Dahl's classic book *The Witches*, which reaches its climax at a convention of witches, *Granny* culminates at a convention of grannies. At the convention, they unveil a new invention intending to use Joe as the guinea pig.

"The Grannymatic Enzyme Extractor!" Elsie Bucket announced, moving into the light. "Last year, you will recall, we tested my elixir of life, the secret potion that would make me and all my dear granny friends young again. Over one hundred ingredients had gone into my elixir of life! Avocado oil, ginseng, yoghurt, royal jelly, raw oysters, ox blood, iron oxide, zinc, milk of magnesia, yak's milk, cactus juice, the yolk of an ostrich egg and much, much more. But it didn't work. And why didn't it work? Because there was one missing ingredient.

"Enzymes are the stuff of life. Without enzymes there can be no life. And this boy's enzymes, added to my wonderful elixir, will turn back the clock and instantly return us to our glorious, wonderful youth! And what about this glorious, wonderful youth?" Elsie Bucket pointed at Joe. "Sadly, the operation will kill the child. But I am sure even he won't mind when he knows how happy he will be making all of us."

"I do mind!" Joe shouted.

Elsie Bucket ignored him. "In a minute I shall flick the switch," she said. "The machine will do the rest. His enzymes will be sucked out of him . . . By the time the process is over," she added almost as an afterthought, "the boy will be as shriveled as an overcooked cocktail sausage. If you find this disturbing, I suggest you don't look." (*Granny* 111–112)

This excerpt shows a wonderful mixture of humor, satire, and horror. Anthony really takes revenge on his own grandmother here. Not only is Granny old, ugly, and mean, she is willing for her own grandchild to die so that SHE can live longer! By blowing up his own grandmother's evil to such epic proportions, Anthony is allowed to laugh at her and be horrified, and thus he comes to terms with her actions.

Joe, of course, survives the Grannymatic Enzyme Extractor, but he must have one final confrontation with his Granny.

Granny took a step nearer. Joe stood his ground . . . "But you can't hurt me any more. I know about you. And one day . . ."

"One day what?" Joe had been too kind, even now, to say what he was thinking. But now Granny said it for him. "One day I'll be dead? Is that what you're thinking?" She smiled toothlessly in the moonlight. Smoke from the ruined building curled around her legs. "Oh, yes. Even I won't live for ever. But don't you see, Joe, you'll never be rid of me. Because, you see, when I die, I'll come back. I'll come back and haunt you and there's nothing you'll be able to do."

"You're lying," Joe whispered.

"Oh, no! The grave won't keep me lying down for long. I'll come back, you'll see. Just when you least expect it . . ." Her eyes blinked, black in the white light of the moon. "And then . . . oh yes, what fun we'll have." (*Granny* 117–118)

Did writing the book allow Anthony to come to terms with his grandmother? Were his childhood feelings toward her the same when he was an adult? Was he able to forgive her? He said:

Well at the end of her life, the last year of her life, after my mother had died of cancer, helped, I have to say, by my grandmother along the way, she was all alone. Let me first say that when my mother became ill, my grandmother's contribution to this was to stress her out as much as she possibly could. "Who's going to do my shopping? You're lying in bed, who's going to come and do my shopping for me?" My mother would drag herself off her sickbed when she was months away from death to go and do the shopping for this woman. But, in the last seven or eight months of my grandmother's life, she was stuck in an old people's home, with nobody to talk to, nobody to visit her, and the only person who went was me. I ended up visiting once a week because it's what my mother would have wanted. And truly there was no hatred left. And then she died, and I thought, why don't I use her? And I still feel proud of the fact that although she never made anybody laugh in life, in the way I portrayed her in the book, she's at last become a joke.[39]

Anthony's considers his next book the most important book of his career. And to this day, it's also his favorite. He said, "If you were to ask me which one is the closest to me (and in a sense the most pivotal) it would be *The Switch*—one of my less known books."[40]

After exploring and satirizing a part of his past in *Granny*, Anthony was ready to move on to *The Switch*, published in 1996. In this book, his writing took on a new confidence not found in his earlier books. He was finding his footing as a writer. He said:

The Switch differs from all my other books only in that the two children at center, Bob Snarley and Tad Spencer are real characters and there is a depth to the writing that hadn't been in my earlier books. It is autobiographical in only the sense that when I was a child, I had always wished to be someone else and this [book] examines what happens when someone becomes someone else.[41]

But perhaps *The Switch* is more autobiographical than even Anthony realizes. While it is true that the book examines what happens when someone (Tad) becomes someone else (Bob), there is more to the book then just that. Elements of Anthony's life are evident in the portrayal of Tad and his parents, Sir Hubert Spencer and Lady Geranium Spencer. As much as he might deny it, it's hard to imagine that parts of Anthony's own life do not emerge in these portraits, starting with Sir Hubert Spencer:

He was a large, imposing man with wavy silver hair and purple blotches in his cheeks, nose and hands. He was dressed, as always, in a plain black suit cut from the very finest material. As he strode into the room and sat down he pulled out an antique pocket watch and glanced at the face.

"Good Evening, Tad," he said. "Good to see you. Now. I can give you nine and a half minutes . . ."

"Gosh! Thank you, Father."

Tad was delighted. He knew that his Father was a busy man. In fact, business ruled his life. (*The Switch* 12–13)

Lady Geranium Spencer also seems familiar:

Tad went over to the swimming pool, where a bored-looking woman was lying on a sunlounger, gazing at herself intently in a small mirror. (*The Switch* 9)

And of course, Tad himself is reminiscent of Anthony as a child:

> As he flicked a page, he popped another cherry marzipan chocolate into his mouth, the fourteenth he had eaten since Ipswich. (*The Switch* 7)
>
> Lady Spencer cast a critical eye at her son. "Have you put on weight?" she asked.
>
> "Just a little, Mumsy. I'm afraid you're going to have to buy me a completely new uniform for next term. This one's much too tight."
>
> "What a bore! That's the third this year."
>
> "I know. The elastic on my underpants snapped during the headmaster's speech. It was rather embarrassing . . ." (*The Switch* 10–11)

Tad owned the best of anything and everything. And yet, although being raised in the lap of luxury in a way that almost everyone dreams of being raised, like Anthony, Tad was not happy with his life.

> Suddenly Snatchmore Hall seemed like a prison to him. His parents, his great wealth, his school and his surroundings were just the shackles that bound him and he wanted none of it.
>
> "I wish I was somebody else," he muttered to himself.
>
> And 127 million light years away, a star that had been burning white suddenly glowed green, just for a few seconds, before burning white again.
>
> But Thomas Arnold David Spencer hadn't seen it. He was already asleep. (*The Switch* 17–18)

Of course, many writers make use of their own lives in their fictions. And the Spencer family is a sketch, or a quick satire of Anthony's family. A rich, distant businessman father. A bored socialite mother. And a spoiled overweight son whose favorite authors are Shakespeare and Dickens. But things were about to become very different for Tad.

> The boy was thin and pale and about a year younger than Tad. He had long fair hair that hung in greasy strands over a rather sickly looking face dotted with acne. His right ear was pierced twice with a silver ring and a stud shaped like a crescent moon. The boy could have been handsome. He had bright blue eyes, full lips and a long, slender neck. But he looked hungry and dirty and there was something about his expression that was pinched and mean. Right now he was standing outside the caravan, staring at Tad through a small window. Tad opened his mouth to cry out. The boy did the same.
>
> And that was when Tad knew, with a sense of terror, that he wasn't looking at a window. He was looking at a mirror. And it wasn't a boy standing outside the caravan. It was his reflection!
>
> *It was him!* (*The Switch* 24–25)

In *The Switch*, Tad switches places with Bob Snarby, the son of Eric and "Doll" Snarby. Tad now lives in a dirty run-down trailer and his parents run a Lucky Numbers stall at a cheap carnival. Doll and Eric are the opposite of his own parents, and equally bad.

> Before him stood a man, wearing a pair of stained pajama trousers but no top. His naked stomach was dangling over the waistband, a nasty rash showing around the belly button. The man's face was pale and bony and covered with a gingery stubble that matched what was left of his hair. His eyes were half-closed. One of them had a sty bulging red and swollen under the lid. There was a cigarette dangling from his lips and Tad realized with a shiver of disgust that he must have slept with it there all night. (*The Switch* 25)

Tad's new mother was no better. In just a few lines, Anthony is able to draw a marvelous portrait of a thoroughly repulsive woman. Note his use of humor and iteration—in this case, a list of words beginning with the same letter, the letter "f".

> She was one of the ugliest women Tad had ever seen. For a start, she was so fat that the caravan rocked when she moved. Her legs, swatched in black stockings, were thin at the ankles but thicker than tree-trunks by the time they appeared into her massive, exploding bottom. She had arms like hams in a butcher's shop and as for her face, it was so fat that it seemed to have swallowed itself. Her squat nose, narrow eyes and bright red lips had sunk into flabby folds of flesh. Her hair was black and tightly permed. She wore heavy plastic earrings, a wooden necklace and a variety of metal bangles, brooches and rings. (*The Switch* 27)

So even though Tad had gotten his wish and become someone else, things have, in a way, gotten even worse. His new parents loan "Bob" (the boy whose body Tad is inhabiting) out to the evil criminal Finn. (Similar to the character of Fagin in Dicken's novel *Oliver Twist*.) Finn uses Tad to help him to break into rich people's houses. Tad, the spoiled child who had never had to do anything or make a decision in his life, was forced to grow up in a hurry.

But there is still more. Not only does Tad have to escape from the criminal element from his new life. He also learns about the criminal basis of his *former* life, and of his father's fortune.

Tad's father, Sir Hubert Spencer, appears to be a thoroughly respectable businessman.

> Ten years ago, Sir Hubert Spencer had set up a chain of shops that now stretched across England, Europe and America. The

shops were simply called "Beautiful World" and sold soaps, shampoos, body lotions, sun creams, vitamins, minerals, herbs and spices . . . everything to make you feel beautiful inside and out. What made these shops special, however, was that the ingredients for many of the products came from the Third World—yak's milk from the mountain villages of Tibet, for example, or crushed orchids from the tropical rain forests of Sumatra. And all the shops carried a notice in large letters in the window:

**NONE OF OUR
PRODUCTS
ARE TESTED ON
ANIMALS** (*The Switch* 13)

He grew to hold much fortune, honor, respectability, and more.

Sir Hubert never stopped. He was always developing new products, finding new ingredients, dreaming up new advertising ideas, selling more products. It was said that while he was being knighted by the queen, two years before, he had managed to sell her ten gallons of face-cream and a lifetime's supply of Japanese seaweed shampoo. He had appeared on the front page of all the newspapers after that. Because, despite his great wealth, Sir Hubert was very popular. "Good old Sir Hubert!" people would shout out if they saw him in the street. "He may be stinking rich, but he's all right." The reasons for this popularity—and also for his knighthood—was his charity work. At about the same time that he had set up Beautiful World he had started a charity called ACID. This stood for The Association for Children in Distress and was based in London.

ACID aimed to help all the young people who had run

away or had been abandoned in the city, giving them shelter and providing them with food or clothes. Tad himself had donated two pairs of socks and a Mars bar to the charity. He was very proud of his father and dreamed of the day when, maybe, he would be knighted too. (*The Switch* 14–15)

The character of Sir Hubert is an exaggerated version of Anthony's own father. While Mark Horowitz was never knighted, he was a successful businessman with government connections. And, as is now known, it is possible that Mark did not earn his fortune by strictly honest means. But how could Anthony write about his own father's flaws? How could he handle this in a work of fiction? Let's take a look.

In his great novel *Bleak House*, Charles Dickens shows the ties that bind the upper and lower classes. In *The Switch*, Anthony shows the same thing. Still trapped in Bob Snarby's body, Tad is sent to his own father's charity, ACID, for assistance. It is here that Tad learns the truth about his father. ACID is a sham. It takes poor, helpless people off the street and puts them into his father's clutches. Because while it is true that none of Beautiful World's cosmetics are tested on animals, Tad learns that they are tested on children.

One boy was dressed only in swimming trunks, standing in an elaborate shower cubicle. The floor was slowly turning and as the boy rotated he was sprayed by different-coloured jets of water. An elderly woman was watching him closely and every few minutes she took a Polaroid photograph, clipping the results to a wall-chart nearby.

Opposite him, a black youth of about eighteen was lying on a bed, completely covered in some sort of pale silver grease. The grease started at his ankles and went all the way to his neck. His eyes were hidden behind a large pair of goggles, obviously designed to protect him from the glowing neon tubes that hung only inches from his skin. Two men in white coats were watching him . . .

There were girls there as well. One was strapped to a high-backed chair, her feet immersed in a large bucket that buzzed and vibrated beneath her. A few metres away from her, a second had been hung upside down with wires attached to her ears and nose. Opposite her, in a partly screened-off area, another boy was being slowly spun in what looked like a giant washing machine, while next to him a girl of about twenty sat in a bath, with green foam bubbling around her neck. (*The Switch* 104–105)

In a salute to Orson Welles's classic film *The Lady in Shanghai*, the climactic scene of *The Switch* takes place back at the carnival in a hall of mirrors. Tad, still trapped in Bob's body, confronts his father (who, of course, does not realize it is his son) with what he knows.

"You want me to tell you the truth?" Sir Hubert called out. "It's my pleasure!" He slammed his hand against a mirror. A thousand hands thundered at a thousand reflections of Tad. "Yes—boy—you have learned rather too much about me. My little experiments in the Centre? How else can I be sure that my products are safe? The stupid public gets all upset when it's rabbits or mice or monkeys on the operating table but who cares about delinquent children dragged off the London streets? Homeless, hopeless children like you? So—yes—my charity, ACID, turned you into a laboratory rat as it has done a hundred children before you. It's all you deserve."

"And you kill people!" Tad cried, horrified and sickened by what he was hearing. "The Arambayans . . ."

"Primitives! Savages! Animals!" Sir Hubert laughed.

"They wouldn't sell me what I wanted so of course I had them wiped out. Do you think anyone cares? When people pay seventeen pounds fifty for a bottle of Moonfruit Massage, they're not thinking of a tribe of Indians on the other side of the world! Nobody ever thinks of anybody else. That's what capitalism is all about!" (*The Switch* 177)

So how did Anthony do it? He did it by utilizing one of the most effective tools in his writing arsenal—exaggeration. By making Sir Hubert such a grotesquely evil man, it enabled him to help deal with his own father's faults, which paled in comparison. Writing was a way to help Anthony deal with his past. By writing about it, by putting it down on paper in a highly exaggerated form, it helped him to put the past in its place and move on.

And, in fact, moving on is one of the main themes of *The Switch*. By the end of the book, Tad and Bob are back in their proper bodies, and are now equals. Tad's parents are in jail, and Bob's parents have disappeared, fleeing the police. Tad and Bob are both living at St. Elizabeth's Institute. And it is here, living on an equal footing, that they are able to become friends, and both can begin new lives.

"So what now?" Bob Snarby asked.

"I hoped we could be friends," Tad said.

"What? You 'n' me?"

"Why not?" Tad sat down next to Bob. "Nobody's ever known each other as well as you and I have. I mean, we've actually been each other."

"Did you ever tell anyone?" Bob Snarby asked.

"About the switch?" Tad shook his head. "No. I didn't think anyone would believe me."

"Me either."

"It's only two years," Tad went on. "And then we'll be on

our own. No parents. No Finn. Nobody to tell us what to do or turn us into what they want us to be. In some ways, maybe that's the best thing that ever happened to me."

"Yeah? And what then?" Bob wasn't convinced. "What do you think will happen to us then? You say you're the same as me now. Well, what chance do you think people like us ever have?"

"I think we can be anything we want to be," Tad replied. "If we stick together. And if we want it hard enough. With what you know and what I know . . . together we can take on the world." (*The Switch* 186–187)

Many heroes of children's literature are parentless. It is the absence of parents that gives the children an opportunity to come into their own. As Anthony put it, "At the end of . . . *The Switch*, two boys who have nothing, and no parents, make a discovery which is the inspiration of all of my books. They discover that they can take on the world and win."[42]

The Switch received great attention from the British press and has since been translated into eight languages besides English. While the book did not sell as well as Anthony had hoped—he has always had high expectations for his sales—, in the end it did not matter as the book is still in print, 10 years after its publication.

Did you know...

Did you know that early in Orlando Bloom's career, he made an appearance in Anthony Horowitz's television series, *Midsomer Murders*? He did! In *Midsomer Murders* Bloom ended up dead with a pitchfork in his chest!

Then it was time for more writing for television. 1997 saw the premiere of two series: *Midsomer Murders* and *Crime Traveller*. *Crime Traveller*, Anthony's first original series for television, was about a detective who is able to travel back in time, and then solve the murders before they actually begin! It took Anthony eight months to write the series: ". . . three months for the first episode, two for the second, then a mad rush to complete the other five. I was writing episodes while finished episodes were already being shot."[43]

Unfortunately for Anthony, although the show developed a cult following, it was not renewed for any additional seasons.

His second series was more popular. *Midsomer Murders* was a mystery series based on the novels of Carolyn Graham. Anthony wrote eight episodes for this successful series.

Anthony's next book, *The Devil and His Boy*, was his first and only historical novel to date. And, interestingly enough—the book was written on a bet! Anthony said:

> This was written as a result of a bet with my publisher. At this time, I had moved to Walker Books and I wanted to prove to them that it would be possible to write a historical novel that actually appealed to children. In a sense I failed because this book has sold far fewer [copies] than anything else I have written, although on the other hand, it was the first book I sold to the USA and [it] began my career with Philomel. People who have read it like it very much and I have a great fondness for it. I have always been a great admirer of the Elizabethan period and love Shakespeare (of course) and Elizabeth is something of a hero of mine. I've always thought that it was one of those books that should perhaps reach a wider audience.[44]

The Devil and His Boy was Anthony's breakthrough to his American audience and it received excellent reviews throughout the United Kingdom. The book plunges the reader directly into the world of Shakespeare and Queen Elizabeth, and was described by *The School Library Journal* as "a rollicking good tale."[45] *Kirkus Reviews* said that Anthony's writing "convincingly portrays the sights, smells, and sounds of lower-class Elizabethan England in 1593."[46]

The novel tells the tale of Tom Falconer, who escapes his village existence to find himself alone and homeless in London. There, he encounters a vibrant assortment of beggars and thieves, actors and assassins, even meeting real historical personages as William Shakespeare and Queen Elizabeth herself!

Anthony knows that the past is nothing like the present, and he is never afraid to show the reader the reality of what living in those times was really like.

The inn stood just outside the town, next to a large swamp. It was a squat, dark, evil-smelling place with rotting timbers and moldy walls. It had few windows—glass was too expensive—but the noise of singing and the smell of roasting meat seeped through the thatched roof and chimney. An inn sign swung in the wind. The sign showed the head of a pig, severed from its body, for that was the inn's name:

THE PIG'S HEAD, FRAMLINGHAM.
PROPRIETORS: SEBASTIAN & HENRIETTA SLOPE.

At about five o'clock in the afternoon a young boy came out of the inn carrying a bucket. Despite the weather, he was wearing only the lightest of clothes: a shirt open at the neck, a waistcoat that was too short for him, a pair of trousers that flapped around his ankles. He had neither shoes nor socks.

His bare feet splashed in the mud as he went to draw water from the well.

The boy was about twelve or thirteen years old. Nobody knew or cared exactly when he had been born. He had long reddish-brown hair, pale skin, and bright, intelligent eyes. He was painfully thin—his rags seemed to hang off his shoulders without actually touching his body—and there was a bruise on the side of his cheek the size of a man's fist. He lowered the bucket into the well, gripping the handle that groaned rustily as it turned; his fingers were unusually long and slender. The boy's name was Thomas Falconer. That, at least, would be the name they'd carve on his gravestone when starvation or the plague carried him away. For now they simply called him Tom. (*The Devil and His Boy* 11–12)

Anthony enjoyed the opportunity to make the Elizabethan era come alive for his readers. He hoped that his love of the age would spark a similar interest among his readers. And of course, he tried to be as accurate as possible, as he pointed out in the book's Afterword.

Whenever possible in *The Devil and His Boy* I've tried to use actual details from the sixteenth century to give the story a ring of truth. Queen Elizabeth did have five quilts on her bed. Dinner at The Pig's Head would have cost you "sixpence downstairs and eightpence up." London boys did enjoy throwing mud-balls at strangers. And so on. (*The Devil and His Boy* 181)

Not to say that Anthony's sense of humor is diminished.

That said, however, it is quite possible that teachers will find some mistakes in this book. These mistakes are entirely deliberate. I put them in to keep the teachers happy. (*The Devil and His Boy* 182)

After the publication of *The Devil and His Boy* in 1999, Anthony turned to the scary stories he and his mothers had shared so many years before. The first collection of stories was called *Horowitz Horror: Nine nasty stories to chill you to the bone*. This was followed two years later by a second collection, *More Horowitz Horror: Eight sinister tales you'll wish you'd never read*.

Horror, of course, had been a long-time fascination for Anthony, and he has very definite ideas on what makes a good horror story:

> The secret of a good horror for kids is not too much violence, that is to say blood letting and sheer nastiness should be at a minimum, and suspense and originality are perhaps the two most important aspects. I like very much writing horror about ordinary objects, like cameras, barns, photo machines at stations, hearing aids. Things one sees everyday and takes for granted. I love the idea that everything and anything can have a darker side.[47]

Indeed, the strongest stories in these collections show the horror in everyday items. In *Light Moves*, a computer formerly owned by a racing correspondent mysteriously gives winning predictions for upcoming horse races. In *The Man With the Yellow Face*, a photo booth's pictures show what the subject will look like in the future. In *The Sound of Murder* a hearing aid hears the thoughts of a murderous French teacher. And in *The Phone Goes Dead*, a cell phone proves to be a link between the living and the dead.

Technology going awry is a major concern in the stories. But, as Anthony points out, he's no Luddite (a person opposed to new technology.) As he says, "I rather like technology, but I also like science fiction films where computers try and kill you or horror stories like Stephen King's *Chris-*

tine, where it's just a car. It just seemed a fertile area to write about."[48]

In between the two collections, Anthony wrote his only play to date, *Mindgame*. The play, a psychological thriller about a serial killer, was set in an insane asylum and after a 16-week tour around the United Kingdom, returned to London where it ran for nine weeks. *Mindgame* received mixed reviews. For instance, the critic for *The Telegraph* called it "genius" and a "highly entertaining schlock show,"[49] while *The London Evening Standard* called it "spectacularly ridiculous,"[50] and *The Times* added that the play was "enjoyably absurd."[51] Anthony commented on the experience of writing a play:

> It was the only play for the stage I have written. It was something of a nightmare experience in that it was very successful out of London, on tour around the country, yet somewhat savaged by at least half the critics in London when it came to the West End. [The West End is the London equivalent of Broadway in New York City.] I should say that half the critics did love it, but not enough to save it and I found the experience very bruising. Normally, people criticize a year or two after [the project is finished] and when I am five or six projects down the line, so their criticisms are unable to touch me. Here it was happening every night in front of me and therefore their criticisms were more hurtful, and I thought, wrong, because I still believe that *Mindgame* was perhaps my most original and innovative piece of work. I don't want to sound arrogant, but that's how I feel and I don't think anything in the theatre is quite like it and I do have a real hope that I will resurface. I have just heard there is to be an off-Broadway version of it, perhaps next year.[52]

The play may not have done as well as Anthony would have liked, but he was willing to chalk it up to experience and move on. Unbeknownst to him, his greatest success was right around the corner.

Although Anthony Horowitz had an active career as a television writer, his dream of becoming a well-known children's author as still unrealized by the end of the 1990s. After Harry Potter came along he decided to make one more go at writing for children before giving up. It is a good thing he did!

Career Crossroads

BY THE END OF THE 1990s, Anthony Horowitz was at a career crossroads. His career as a television writer was thriving. His career as a children's book author was not. Although he had written children's books in many styles and genres, none of them had reached the kind of audience he had been hoping for. Children's books themselves were still considered something of a "minor" market. But then along came a young wizard named Harry Potter, and the game changed completely.

Indeed, Harry changed everything when it came to children's books. The huge sales of the Harry Potter titles (as well as the success of the movies and everything else "Harry") reminded publishers that there was a gigantic market to be reached. And

J.K. Rowling's success helped to inspire other authors. After all, if she could write terrific, exciting books, AND achieve great success, why couldn't they? And as it turns out, Harry Potter is directly responsible for the creation of Alex Rider. Anthony says:

> I was thinking about writing a third *Groosham Grange* I started hearing that there was a book that was very similar to the first *Groosham Grange* that was doing spectacularly well. And I heard rumors of film deals and all sorts of things, so I went out to read Harry Potter and was a little more puzzled than anything else, because it did strike me as remarkably similar in many ways. Then things got weirder with the second Harry Potter book and the whole thing really took off. I was getting letters asking if I was going to sue her, especially from France, where *Groosham* was always popular. But my feeling about Harry Potter was always the same from the start, that it was a coincidence. I never thought for a minute that J.K. had deliberately set out and stolen ideas from me. Besides which, I always thought that *Groosham Grange* One and Two were very light silly books, and Harry Potter was a whole world which is why it succeeded. So it never ever for a single second crossed my mind that I should take any sort of action or feel aggrieved or bothered, really. But what it did make me think was that I should do something completely different. I remember again the moment when I sat down and said (to myself) what I will do is sit down and write a children's book that doesn't have any of the jokes of *Granny* or *Groosham Grange*, none of those little puns. I will write a character who is not one of my knockabout characters who has no inner life. I will write a much more seriously considered character and his name will be Alex Rider and he will be a fourteen year old spy.[53]

And Alex was a 14-year-old spy who changed everything for Anthony. With Alex, Anthony's writing took on a new seriousness, a new intensity and urgency. Readers were presented with a new kind of character for Anthony, one they could actually care about.

> He entered the house through the kitchen, the same way he had left it the night before. It was only eight o'clock, but the whole place seemed to be deserted. He ran up the staircase and along the corridor to his room on the first floor. Slowly, he opened the door. It seemed his luck was holding out. There was nobody there. Without turning on the light, he went inside and snatched up the telephone. The line was dead. Never mind. He found the cartridges for his Game Boy, his yo-yo, and the zit cream and crammed them into his pockets. He had already decided not to stay here. It was too dangerous. He would find somewhere to hide out. Then he would use the Nemesis cartridge to contact M16.
>
> He went back to the door and opened it. With a shock he saw Mr. Grin standing in the hallway, looking hideous with his white face, his ginger hair, and his mauve twisted smile. Alex reacted quickly, striking out with the heel of his right hand. But Mr. Grin was quicker. He ducked to one side, then his hand shot out, the side of it driving into Alex's throat. Alex gasped for breath but none came. The butler made an inarticulate sound and lashed out a second time. Alex got the impression that behind the livid scars he really was grinning, enjoying himself. He tried to avoid the blow, but Mr. Grin's fist hit him square on the jaw. He was spun into the bedroom, falling backward.
>
> He never even remembered hitting the floor. (*Stormbreaker* 176–177)

About his idea for *Stormbreaker* Anthony said, "As a child I fantasized about being a spy. I would dream that I wasn't a pudgy 12-year old listening to a dreary French teacher, but that this was my cover and in reality after school I would slip out and save the world."[54]

So where does Alex's character come from? James Bond is the obvious source of inspiration. Created by British author Ian Fleming, English superspy James Bond came to life first in a series of successful novels. Even more popular were the movies, initially starring Sean Connery as Bond, followed by George Lazenby, Roger Moore, Timothy Dalton, and Pierce Brosnan, with Daniel Craig being named as the newest Bond in the fall of 2005. Since the release of the first film, *Dr. No* in 1962, audiences worldwide have been enthralled by the adventures of Agent 007—young Anthony was no exception. The "cool" of Bond, the nifty gadgets, the evil villains—all have contributed to making the Bond films one of the most successful and long running series of films in the history of movies.

It was the idea of transforming James Bond into a cool 14-year-old boy that was Anthony's stroke of genius. According to him, Bond's glamour translates perfectly to the 14-year-old psyche. Anthony said:

> Bond had his cocktails, the car and the clothes. Kids are just

Did you know...

Did you know that the creator of James Bond, Ian Fleming, was also a successful children's book author? Fleming is also the author of the children's classic, *Chitty Chitty Bang Bang.*

as picky. It's got to be the right Nike trainers (sneakers), the right skateboard. And I genuinely think that 14-year-olds are the coolest people on the planet. It's this wonderful, golden age, just at the cusp of manhood when everything seems possible.[55]

Indeed, the 14-year-old boy, the son of a friend, was a partial model for Alex. The boy's name actually is Alex and he really does speak two languages fluently. He, like Alex, does Tai Chi. And Alex (the person) even looks like Alex (the character)!

Anthony's publisher loved the idea of a young spy, and Anthony was ready to write. After all, he had been dreaming about teenage spy adventures for almost his entire life. Alex was, in effect, a character just waiting to be discovered. As Anthony remembered, ". . . once I started writing the first Alex Rider, I knew in my heart that I'd got it right. There was a sense of energy, a sense of this being a real boy."[56]

Alex and Anthony were, even from the beginning, a perfect match. And Anthony knew it:

I did know that *Stormbreaker* would be a success. As I was writing it, I felt there was a new energy in the writing, and something in me that I hadn't discovered before. The character of Alex leapt, fully developed, on to the page.[57]

He commented:

Rider leapt onto the page from the very first sentence. "When the phone rings at three o'clock in the morning, it's never good news." Very very Ian Fleming, that voice of information and authority. And I knew from that time that my life was going to change.[58]

Everything Anthony knew about writing came together in

Stormbreaker: characterization, plot, his sense of adventure, and pace. As Wendy Cooling, children's book consultant put it, Anthony's narrative gift is like J.K. Rowling's in one respect: "They never pause for breath, there is always something happening around the next corner."[59] "There are times," mentions *Booklist* reviewer Jean Franklin, "when a grade-B adventure is just the ticket for a bored teenager, especially if it offers plenty of slam-bang action, spying, and high-tech gadgets."[60]

Stormbreaker, as well as the succeeding Alex Rider titles, do just that. They take their readers on an exciting thrill ride. The first book sets the groundwork for the works that follow. In *Stormbreaker* we first meet 14-year-old Alex Rider, an orphan, being raised by his Uncle Ian. Ian is killed in a car accident, but Alex has doubts that it was accidental, especially after he discovers that the car was riddled with bullet holes. After his curiosity about his uncle's death nearly gets him killed, Alex learns the truth about his Uncle Ian. It turns out, Uncle Ian had been an agent for British intelligence.

The agency asks for Alex's help. Since Alex is already in danger, knowing too much about his uncle's death, he decides that joining the agency might be the best way of keeping himself alive. So Alex leaves prep school for two weeks of intensive training, at the end of which he is given a collection of ultra-cool spy gadgets (a motorized yoyo useful for climbing; acne medicine that eats through metal; and a Game Boy that can be used as a fax/photocopier, an X-ray device, an eavesdropping machine, a bug finder, and a smoke bomb). Fully equipped, Alex sets out on his first assignment.

His first job is to infiltrate a group run by an insane, vengeful inventor named Herod Sayle. Herod has launched an evil plot to kill all the schoolchildren in England using biological weapons, introduced through an in-school computer system called "Stormbreaker." Alex, of course, stops him just in the nick of time, and his career as a spy is begun. Noting that "satirical names abound . . . and the hard-boiled language is equally outrageous," a *Publisher's Weekly* reviewer wrote that "these exaggerations only add to the fun" for readers.[61] *Stormbreaker* was also deemed "an excellent choice for reluctant readers" by *School Library Journal* contributor Lynn Bryant due to its "short cliff-hanger chapters and its breathless pace."[62]

Stormbreaker was an immediate success and a new literary star was born. And a good thing too. If *Stormbreaker* had not done well, Anthony had been ready to throw in the towel on his children's book career. He said:

> When I was doing the Alex Rider book, the books I'd done for Walker had been so-so successful, whilst my other [television] career was flying. My wife Jill said, "Why are you still doing children's books?" and I said to her "Watch what happens to Alex Rider, this is going to be totally different. This is the one." I don't want to sound arrogant, but I knew that this was it. And if it wasn't I would have stopped after Alex Rider. That would have been it.
>
> The first book did better then the others, but then the ball began to roll. Critics began to talk about it, film rights were sold . . . the second book came out . . . and the whole thing just took off.[63]

The second book in the series, *Point Blank* was even more exciting. In it, Alex finds himself sent to a private boarding school in the Alps to investigate the goings on of its headmaster, the South African Dr. Grief. (To escape the school and get help, Alex is forced to snowboard down the Alpine

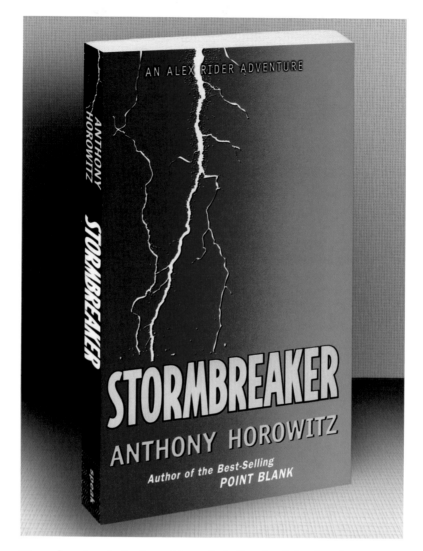

Stormbreaker is Anthony Horowitz's first book in the Alex Rider series. The book created quite a splash when it was published in 2000. Stormbreaker's down-to-earth, realistic, 14-year-old character Alex Rider took young readers into a world of nonstop adventure.

mountain at night on an ironing board, cut to shape using a diamond edged CD popped into his specially made disc-man.) As a *Kirkus Reviews* critic assured readers, "Horowitz devises a string of miraculous circumstances that keep Alex alive and spying throughout."[64] Propelled by hidden passages, frightening medical experiments, and a protagonist who barely stays one step away from death, *Point Blank* was described by Franklin as a "non-stop thriller" in her *Booklist* review.[65]

Adventure after adventure followed, with a new Alex Rider novel appearing annually. Again and again, Alex manages to save the world, using nothing but his own courage and ingenuity (aided, of course, by a constant stream of new and more inventive gadgets). In *Skeleton Key*, Alex is sent to Cuba where a retired Russian general plans to set off a nuclear device, and ultimately, take over the Russian government and restore the lost Soviet empire. In *Eagle Strike,* Alex has to stop his old enemy, renowned assassin Yassen Gregorovich, working for British pop star/peace activist/philanthropist Sir. Damien Cray from using nuclear weapons in a battle that ends on the U.S. presidential jet, Air Force One. And, in *Scorpia*, Alex is temporarily recruited by the evil criminal organization, Scorpia, before being brought back to M16 and stopping Scorpia's evil plot.

Each of the Alex Rider books provides exciting adventures, exotic locations, evil villains, and spy toys beyond belief. (Among the most intriguing inventions supplied to Alex by M16's Mr. Smithers are: exploding bubblegum; a diamond earring that also works as a grenade; a Harry Potter book—Anthony's own little joke—that has a stun dart guy built into the spine; and a missile launching bicycle.)

But it is Alex himself who keeps readers coming back for more. Smart, confident, and self reliant—Alex is the kind of kid that others would like to be like. And even though he always triumphs in the end, he's no superman. He is vulnerable. Readers care about what happens to him. Which is just how his creator wants it. As Anthony remarked, "I'm trying to make Alex credible—so you never lose sight of the fact that he's a flesh and blood 14-year-old boy."[66]

And unlike James Bond, Alex can get hurt. This is intentional on Anthony's part. As he pointed out, "What the Bond films lack . . . is a sense of danger. When you watch a Pierce Brosnan film, you never for a moment believe he might be hurt."[67] Not so with Alex Rider. He screams, faints, and gets his bones broken. He even, at the end of *Scorpia*, gets left for dead, shot by a sniper. (Not to worry though, a new Alex Rider adventure has been published in the United Kingdom and is scheduled to publish in the United States in the spring of 2006.)

But, as frightening as Alex's adventures are, perhaps even scarier is the attitude of his handlers back at M16. To them, Alex is just one more "tool" to use in their neverending battle against evil and darkness. They want to keep him alive as long as he is useful to them. Beyond that, they do not care about him. And since Alex knows this, it adds poignancy to his desire for a normal life. A desire that almost any reader, despite their fascination with the dangerous side of Alex's life, can appreciate.

Anthony was thrilled with Alex's popularity. He had finally achieved the major success in children's books that had so long eluded him. Alex was rapidly becoming one of the most popular literary characters among young readers. But with success came greater responsibility—a legion of fans that Anthony did not want to disappoint. How was Anthony going to keep the series fresh and exciting? How could he continue to come up with keep-you-at-the-edge-of-your-seat plots? How could he continue to keep his readers coming back for more?

With the Alex Rider series, plot is everything. Anthony put it like this:

> When you work in television there is a technical phrase that you use—what is the **locomotive** of this program? The locomotive is basically the machine that moves everything forward, the characters and the events. As long as the locomotive is thundering down the track at 500 miles an hour we're all going to be on board and go with it. But as soon as that locomotive stops at every station to look at the view, people can get off! The locomotive in Alex Rider is the plot, the story, the danger, the suspense. I just keep making sure it never stops until the end of the book. That's how I try to hold on to the reader.[68]

But of course, a great plot requires a great villain. For Anthony, it all starts there. "I normally start with the villain, his motivation, the core of it and build around from there."[69]

Even that is just a beginning. In a 2002 interview, Anthony described in great detail his working process:

> I plan very carefully. The process is this: I start with a core idea. The core idea for *Skeleton Key* was that a nuclear holocaust was caused in Russia to allow the villain to take power. The incident that gave me the idea was the story about the Kirsk submarine. (Authors note: A Russian nuclear powered submarine that sank in 2000 after a series of explosions, killing 118 crewmen.) In that incident the Russian President very nearly lost power—so that gave me the idea. That's the core idea—after that, I draw up a list of ingredients. It's a bit like being a chef and going shopping for ingredients. When I'm making a book, I need some exciting ingredients. I thought pretty early on about the climax with the crane and the submarine—that's one ingredient. [Alex uses a magnetic

crane to lift a nuclear bomb from the submarine and thwart General Sarov's evil plans.] I knew I was going to involve the CIA. And with sports, I thought—let Alex do some surfboarding—we haven't had surfboarding yet so we can have a surfboarding chapter. Then because the books are moving forward a month at a time, [Each book in the series takes place approximately one month after the previous title.] and I realized it was going to be July, I thought we could have Wimbledon [The English tennis championship that take place annually in July] as an ingredient. So you build the book up with ingredients as being the exciting bits. And then what I do is draw up a structure—a detailed structure, which is sixteen or seventeen chapters. I know what every chapter's going to contain. I know that if chapter four is going to have lots of talking then chapters three and five had to be exciting action chapters and then readers don't have a chance to get bored. If chapter seven is a funny, silly chapter, then I'll make sure that chapter eight is a serious one. That way it's nice and varied. I do lots of doodles as well. And when I plan a television program structure it's very, very detailed: I can't start writing until every single minute of a two hour detective show is planned out—every single scene, every single prop, every clue.[70]

The lessons that Anthony learned from Charles Dickens serve him well in the Rider series: how to pace the storytelling, alternating "talking" and "action" chapters, always looking for ways to keep an reader's interest. He even got pointers on how to *name* his characters from his literary idol. As he mentioned in the same 2002 interview:

Names are difficult; it takes a lot of time to come up with them. I like names that tell you something about the character before you've even met them. It's a technique that my favorite writer, the nineteenth century novelist Charles Dickens used. So when you meet a character in *David Copperfield* called Uriah Heap, you know he's not going to be a nice guy—there's going to be something creepy about him. Wackford Squeers, the name of headmaster [He appears in the Dickens novel *Nicholas Nickleby*.] is the same sort of idea. I also like to use names that tell you something and also have the right sound for them. Sabina Pleasure is obviously a silly one—that's a jokey name. So was Fiona Friend in *Point Blank*. It's like the tradition in James Bond films of having women with funny names like Tiffany Case. Other names are more sinister. In *Skeleton Key*, General Sarov's name came to me when I was reading about sarum, a terrible poison that Japanese terrorists used on the railway system. So sarum became Sarov. His name was originally going to be Skeletov, but that was too silly. Dr. Grief in *Point Blank* is another obvious one—Grief is such a good name. Sometimes I take names out of newspapers. And I put people I meet into books—if I like you, you could well end up in my next book. That's how it works.[71]

Okay. So Anthony has a plot. He has his characters, and they are all named. But part of the fun of the Alex Rider series is following Alex around the world to exotic and exciting cities and locations. How does Anthony do his research? Is he an armchair traveler, going through travel books and the internet to do his research? Not by a long shot. As he said in that 2002 interview, "I have been to virtually all the locations in the books. I've just come back from Amsterdam where Alex is chased in the next book [*Eagle Strike*]. He's given a gadget filled bicycle by Mr. Smithers."[72] [Mr. Smithers is one of the most beloved characters in the Alex Rider series. He's eccentric, funny, and appears to be the only person working in British intelligence who actually cares for Alex.] When the bike arrives, Smithers has attached the following note:

Dear Alex,

I'm probably going to get a roasting for this, but I don't like the idea of you taking off on your own without any backup. This is something I've been working on for you and you might as well have it now. I hope it comes in handy.

Look after yourself, dear boy. I'd hate to hear that anything lethal had happened to you.

All the best,

Smithers

P.S. This letter will self-destruct ten seconds after it comes into contact with the air, so I hope you read it quickly! (*Eagle Strike* 96–97)

Anthony continues:

And I've also been down to the South of France . . . because Alex is thrown into a bull ring with a bull—so I had to go to a bullfight and watch that. For *Skeleton Key*, I have indeed been to Havana, a long time ago. [It is legal for British citizens to travel to Cuba. American citizens are not allowed to go, except under extraordinary circumstances.] I wasn't able to go to Murmansk, but I did speak to people who had been and looked at pictures and books. If I can't go to the locations myself, I read and talk to people.[73]

Going there is one thing. But getting it down on paper is quite another. How does Anthony give his readers a sense of place, without boring them half to death? Anthony says:

How to make it feel that you've been there or make it alive in the book? Well, I've learned that "less is more." The less you write about a place the more people will feel they know it. You need one or two details that persuade the reader that you have been there; something that just says "this person knows." If you write a whole page describing, let us say, Murmansk in Russia, first of all it's going to bore the readers because they want to read about the adventures of Alex not a travel book—they can get that somewhere else. And secondly, it's not going to be very persuasive. If you write a page saying the shops look like this and the buses are a certain color and the train comes from that particular station, people will realize that you are trying too hard. But on the other hand if you just mention a little detail—that a yellow police car goes past—the reader says hang on, police cars aren't yellow—perhaps that's what it's like in Russia. A little detail, well chosen, does more than a whole paragraph of boring description.[74]

So now nearly everything is in place. After setting up the plot and characters, and researching the locations, there's still one thing left for Anthony to investigate. He has to thoroughly research the physical reality of the action and the plot itself. And in this arena, Anthony goes to great lengths for authenticity and believability. The training techniques used in *Stormbreaker* are real. The nanotechnology used in *Scorpia* is real. Anthony says, "I used the internet to research weaponry, but I also talked to a scientist who asked for his name not to be put in, because the terrorist application of nanotechnology is so scary."[75] He climbed the actual 150-meter-high crane operated by Alex in *Point Blank*—even though Anthony is terrified of heights. Even his kids get into the act. For *Point Blank*, Nicholas, then 12 years old, tried snowboarding. And the entire family recently traveled to Peru to research the latest Alex Rider novel. The books are obviously a family affair.

And, when Anthony is finally ready to sit down and write (out of the seven months it normally takes him to write, three months are dedicated to research), he has the perfect hideaway to do it. He says:

> I have a studio in my garden where I work and inside my studio there is nothing but work. [In his studio, Anthony is watched over by a cardboard figure of Alex Rider. And, the skull that his mother gave him for his 13th birthday sits on his desk. It's there to remind him, as he says, "not to waste time."[76]] There are no comforts there. I have my computer, my books and research material, my dog, a bottle of whiskey— that's for the dog. I'm very isolated there—I like that. I have peace and quiet with a view of the garden. I don't have any real routine; I just go to my studio and start writing. When I work, I immerse myself to such an extent that I could start at 10:00 in the morning and when I look up it will be teatime [4:00 in the afternoon is traditionally teatime in Great Britain] and I won't have noticed. But sometimes I might not start until 3:00 in the afternoon—if I don't feel like working in the morning. I write when I want to write.[77]

But it is not often that Anthony does not feel like writing. Typically, Anthony works 10 hour days. Writing is, for him, a passion. He says, "I write like I breathe. It is without a choice or thought about it or being able to stop."[78]

It is a good thing that Anthony enjoys writing so much. As with any writer, getting a rough draft down on paper is only the first step. It is in the process of rewriting that the true book emerges. He says:

> When I write, I write by longhand first; I scribble out on a pad. [Not only does Anthony write his books out first in long hand, he uses an old-fashioned fountain pen, using blue ink!] And then I go to the computer. So already when I go from

handwriting to the computer, I'm making one change. What I'm actually doing is reading what I've written. To my ear it's like a piece of music—I can hear if the writing is good or not. For example, if I wrote the sentences, "Alex marched into the room, he marched to the table and sat down. It was March and it was raining." I've used march three times already, twice for marching into the room and once for the month. I know that's not rhythmic, you don't want to hear the word march three times. Instead I could write "Alex marched into the room and sat down. It was spring and it was raining." I make little changes like that. Sentences need to have a balance and rhythm. One of the joys of reading Jane Austen [British novelist, 1775–1817, best known for her novels *Pride and Prejudice* and *Emma*, among others] is that her sentences are almost like songs, they're so beautifully written. I hope the sentences in my books are like that.

Here's one: "The saloon cabin was rectangular with a wooden floor partially covered by a carpet that has been rolled back, presumably to avoid blood stains." It's not a brilliant sentence but it is nicely balanced. It finishes with blood stains, which is much better than if I had said: "The saloon cabin was rectangular and to avoid blood stains the carpet had been pulled back to reveal a wooden floor." You can see it is less powerful. In the first sentence you are driven forward to the blood stains. I like that energy.[79]

Energy is what young people want to feel. Whether through their music, video games or action movies, young people want to feel a blast of energy, a jolt of excitement in their entertainment. A main character that readers care about, memorably evil villains, great stunts, and exciting locations, are all good, but movies can provide the same things, with a great immediacy. So, how can a writer keep audiences coming back? How can they write a book that young readers want to read, given greater competition for their attention? How does Anthony compete? Of his technique he says:

> I have this belief that young people today have a lot of choices. They've got computer games, thirty odd channels of television [American television can provide hundreds of channels.], cool gear to go outside and play and HOMEWORK. There are a lot of pressures on young people's time. Therefore I feel that when you open a book, a hand should reach out and grab you by the throat and not let go until the very end of the book. Everytime I write anything, I try to keep that hand around your throat. So I have to have a first sentence in every book that will grab you.
>
> I've got *Point Blank* here. "Michael J. Roskoff was a careful man." It's not a great sentence but nonetheless it does invite you to read a bit more. Why is he careful? What is he afraid of? What's going to happen to him? This is an adventure book so you'll want to know how long he is going to survive. If you have read the book, you'll know it's about eight pages before he'll be murdered. Every chapter MUST end with a hook of some sort, not to finish the chapter but to make you feel you must read the next one as something even more exciting is going to happen. Every book has to end with the promise of yet another book to come. So, it's this idea of never letting go. I'm trying to make sure there are no boring bits—no long descriptions, just story, story, story.[80]

Readers were devouring Alex Rider books as fast as Anthony could write them. They were also rediscovering his earlier works, which he felt was particularly gratifying. Finally, he had achieved the level of success as a children's author that he had always dreamt of. And while other writers might be content and satisfied, and begin to take it a little easier, Anthony was not about to stop. He was just entering the busiest period of his career.

In 2005, Anthony Horowitz sits down with boys from Dulwich College,
a private school for boys in England. Anthony loves to be out with his fans.
He spoke to the crowd, encouraged their enthusiasm for reading, answered
questions, and signed books for students in grades 5, 6, and 8.

The Busiest Writer in England

SINCE THE AGE OF 8, Anthony Horowitz had dreamed of being a writer. And finally in the year 2000, at the age of 45, he had reached the level of success in children's literature that he had always wanted. But, once you reach that level, does your drive for success fade? Can you still write with the same passion? Can you write without passion to begin with? Anthony does not think you can:

> I have always found that if I don't enjoy writing, then I can't write. I have to write with total passion. This is a piece of advice I often give to writers—if you are not passionate about your writing, if it feels like hard work and you are bored with—it will come out as

97

a boring piece of writing. If you write with passion and energy and love, the reader at the other end of the process will feel the passion and read with energy and love. Every book I have loved writing, and the most recent books are the ones that I have most enjoyed, so far.[81]

It is good that Anthony still writes with passion and a sense of enjoyment. Because more than 25 years after publishing his first book, he is busier than ever. Since the year 2000, he has been a one man writing machine.

In 2002, Anthony created and wrote the first of five seasons (the sixth is on its way!) of the television series *Foyle's War*, a dramatic mystery series set in southern England during World War II, which has won a British Academy of Film and Television Arts (BAFTA) award and has been in the top-10 dramas since its inception. That year, his first adult novel, *The Killing Joke*, came out to good reviews. (*The Irish Examiner* said it was "Extraordinarily witty . . . utterly original as well as laugh-out-loud funny . . . Horowitz's novel really is a gem."[82]) He wrote the screenplay for the film *The Gathering* starring Christina Ricci. He wrote the screenplay for the movie *Stormbreaker*, the first movie based on an Alex Rider novel. He is currently writing a new series of novels, The Gatekeepers, which he describes as "Stephen King for kids."[83] And of course, there are the Alex Rider books.

Anthony is particularly excited about the possibilities of the The Gatekeepers series. Originally written in the 1980s as The Power of Five series, he is actually—while keeping the same basic plotline of the struggle between good and evil—reworking and rewriting all four books.

The first book in the new series, retitled *Raven's Gate*, was released in the United States in 2005 to excellent reviews:

In 2000, Anthony Horowitz wrote the play Mindgame which
ran at the Vertigo Theatre Factory that fall and at the Vaudeville
Theatre in London's West End. The play ran only nine weeks
in London's theater district but it remains one of Anthony's
favorite works.

Novels about boys (and girls) facing dark forces are nothing new, and this one certainly contains elements of familiar stories (Hello, Harry Potter). But the real-world setting gives this an extra fission of horror, and Horowitz's vivid descriptions are not for the fainthearted. It's what inside all the thrills, however, that makes the book so strong: characters that readers will care about and root for. There will be an eager audience for the next in the series, to be titled *Evil Star*.[84]

Not many authors go back and have the opportunity to redo or "repair" their earlier works. What inspired Anthony to do so?

For one thing, current events inspired Anthony to revisit his earlier works. "It struck me that this was the right time, and a good time, to explore the idea of good versus evil—principally around the issue of war in Iraq—and the idea of corruption in high places which is not only unworthy but, given what has happened in Iraq, quite evil."[85]

There was more to it than that. Because they were written early in his career, Anthony was interested in looking at them to evaluate them based on the writer he had become. He said:

The books did moderately well and twenty-something years later I revisited them to see if there was anything there that I could keep. I seemed to remember that although the writing was only average, some of the ideas were quite good, particularly in the first two books. I reread them, decided to polish them, just as an experiment really, and ended up completely re-writing them, by which I mean 70% of the material is new. To my surprise, Philomel books [his American publisher] turned them down, a mistake they have come very much to regret. The books then went to auction and were bought for a large sum of money by Scholastic. Rewriting the books has been very interesting, to revisit myself aged 24 (or 25 I think) to see how good I was in some areas and how bad in others. It is very interesting to listen to your early voice.[86]

And of course, besides The Gatekeepers series, Alex Rider casts a huge shadow, and even, Anthony confesses, somewhat influenced the character of Matt in *Raven's Gate*. Anthony said, "It's quite hard to feel into another character when I've got Alex Rider sitting on my shoulder."[87] Understandable perhaps, and with five Alex Rider titles written, and the sixth, entitled *Ark Angel*, to be published in the United States in April of 2006, it is now the longest continuing series of books that Anthony has written. As with any series of books, the challenges for the writer increase with each new book. Does each book get easier or harder to write? How do you continue to keep yourself interested in writing them? Anthony explains:

> The books are both easier and more difficult to write as I continue. They are easier because there are so many characters that I know and so much history that I can draw on, that a certain richness develops on it's own without me having to search for it. Mrs. Jones, Blunt, Smithers, all these people know Alex now. They have a relationship with him and there is so much more for me to explore. More difficult, why? Because how many more stunts are there, how many more stunts can I invent, how many more pieces of action can I think up that haven't already been done in books or in James Bond books. So coming up with new ideas and having each idea fresh and original and as good, if not better than the one before becomes increasingly difficult.
>
> [Interestingly], the series has become perhaps darker than I had imagined, particularly in *Scorpia* . . . I wouldn't go back and change anything . . . but I was careful in *Ark Angel* to lighten the tone and make the adventure more cheerful, to try

and end the feeling of darkness that had come in *Eagle Strike* and in *Scorpia*.[88]

Anthony does foresee a time, though, when he will end the Alex Rider series. He said:

> I can't see there being more than two more. Obviously with the film franchise developing, everyone hopes for more and more, but I very much believe in [not] outstaying one's welcome. I don't want to start producing books that are just a faint echo of themselves. I do have a plot in my head for the next one and I have a feeling that [there] is another book after that, but beyond that I don't know.[89]

And of course, there are the films. Many writers without film experience have to turn their books over to professional screenwriters, and hope for the best. Not Anthony. With his experience, he was asked to write the screenplay himself. This gives him at least a certain amount of control, and although not all of his film experiences have been good ones, he is cautiously optimistic about the film about which he said:

> I think it's going to be a very good film and I am excited and I think it really could work, you never know. But as I sit here, two weeks into filming, all the signs are good. Writing the screenplay was fascinating. Having to throw out so much

Did you know...

Did you know that Anthony Horowitz is considering writing a new book using a new name and identity? He thinks that because he has become so famous, it would be interesting to see what the reaction would be like if he published a book and nobody knew he was the author.

action—there was too much for the film. Having to work it and rework it over fourteen different drafts and having to create something that was very similar to the books and yet at the same time something very different. Something that would be true to the world I had created and yet would serve the demand . . . of everybody . . . involved in the production.[90]

But of course Anthony is more than just an extraordinarily busy writer. He is now a celebrity. He has the level of success as a children's writer that he has always wanted. Is it enough to satisfy him? Anthony said:

> I've been anonymous for most of my career. That's been one of the great things about it that nobody knew I was there. That's why I've managed to dabble in television and in radio, and in theatre, the works. If I'd written Alex Rider when I was 25, I'd be the one who writes spy stories. In retrospect, anonymity has been wonderful. I'm not complaining. I had a dream that there was something at the end of the rainbow, but I'm not sure I've actually found it yet.[91]

So it is that search for the unnamable, that something just beyond the horizon, as well as his passion for writing that keeps Anthony going. And that is a good thing for his legion of young fans. As long as he is searching, as long as his passion continues, he will keep writing. He said:

> For me all that I ever wanted to do is to write. And I've always loved writing. And I still love it as much as I ever did, except now everyone's enjoying it too. It's fun.[92]

1 Kate Kellaway, "Boy's Own Hero," *The Guardian*, April 10, 2005.

2 Dennis Abrams's email interview with Anthony Horowitz, July 28, 2005.

3 Alec, "An interview with Anthony Horowitz," *Write Away! Meets Anthony Horowitz, http://improbability.ultralab.net/writeaway/anthonyhorowitz.htm.*

4 Amanda Craig, "An Interview with Anthony Horowitz," *www.amandacraig.com/pages/journalism/interviews/anthony_horowitz.htm.*

5 Anthony Horowitz, "Perils of Privilege," *Evening Standard*, March 24, 2003.

6 Barry Forshaw, "Anthony Horowitz: Growing up in public," *The Independent*, August 13, 2004.

7 Dennis Abrams's email interview with Anthony Horowitz, July 28, 2005.

8 Ibid.

9 Sarah Crompton, "I Knew that Alex Was Special From The Start," *The Telegraph*, March 30, 2005.

10 Barry Farshaw, "Anthony Horowitz: Growing up in public."

11 Penguin Group (Canada), "Biography of Anthony Horowitz," Penguin Books Authors, *www.penguin.ca/nf/Author/AuthorPage/0,,0_1000015379,00.html.*

12 Dennis Abrams's email interview with Anthony Horowitz, July 28, 2005.

13 Ibid.

14 Ibid.

15 Ibid.

16 Penguin Group (Canada), "Biography of Anthony Horowitz."

17 Anthony Horowitz, "Perils of Privilege."

18 Danuta Kean, "Anthony Horowitz talks to Danuta Kean about sick jokes," *www.orionbooks.co.uk/interview.aspx?ID=10964.*

19 Anthony Horowitz, "Alex Rider: Frequently Asked Questions," *www.anthonyhorowitz.com/alexrider/faq/index.html.*

20 Danuta Kean, "Anthony Horowitz talks to Danuta Kean about sick jokes."

21 Dennis Abrams's email interview with Anthony Horowitz, July 28, 2005.

22 Ibid.

23 Danuta Kean, "Anthony Horowitz talks to Danuta Kean about sick jokes."

24 Barry Forshaw, "Anthony Horowitz: Growing up in public."

25 Kate Kellaway, "Boy's Own Hero."

26 Dennis Abrams's phone interview with Anthony Horowitz, August 31, 2005.

27 Ibid.

28 "Biography of Anthony Horowitz," *Contemporary Authors* (Farmington Hills, MI: Thomson Gale, 2004).

29 Anthony Horowitz, "Perils of Privilege."

30 Dennis Abrams's email interview with Anthony Horowitz, July 28, 2005.

31 Kate Weisman, *Booklist* (Chicago, IL: American Library Association, 2004).

32 Dennis Abrams's email interview with Anthony Horowitz, July 28, 2005.

33 Alec, "An interview with Anthony Horowitz."

34 Dennis Abrams's email interview with Anthony Horowitz, July 28, 2005.

35 Ibid.

36 Dennis Abrams's phone interview with Anthony Horowitz, August 31, 2005.

37 Dennis Abrams's email interview with Anthony Horowitz, July 28, 2005.

38 Dennis Abrams's phone interview with Anthony Horowitz, August 31, 2005.

39 Ibid.

40 Dennis Abrams's email interview with Anthony Horowitz, May 27, 2005.

41 Dennis Abrams's email interview with Anthony Horowitz, July 28, 2005.

42 Nicolette Jones, "A Schoolboy James Bond is Busy Saving the World," *The Times* (of London), September 11, 2001.

43 "Background about Time Traveller," The Crime Traveller Homepage, September 2005, *www.crimetraveller.co.uk/background.asp?css=yonb*.

44 Dennis Abrams's email interview with Anthony Horowitz, July 28, 2005.

45 Barbara Scotto, "Review of The Devil and His Boy," *School Library Journal* (New York, NY: Reed Business Information, Inc., 2000).

46 Kirkus Reviews, "Review of The Devil and His Boy" (New York, NY: Kirkus Associates, L.P., 1999), *www.amazon.com/gp/product/product-description/0698119134/ref=dp_prod-desc_0/103-5847675-1779802?%5Fencoding=UTF8&n=283155*.

47 Dennis Abrams's email interview with Anthony Horowitz, July 28, 2005.

48 Ibid.

49 "Mindgame on stage in London's West End Vaudeville Theatre," London Theatre Guide, *www.albemarle-london.com/mindgame.html*.

50 Ibid.

51 Ibid.

52 Dennis Abrams's email interview with Anthony Horowitz, July 28, 2005.

53 Dennis Abrams's phone interview with Anthony Horowitz, August 31, 2005.

54 Nicolette Jones, "A Schoolboy James Bond is Busy Saving the World."

55 Penguin Group (Canada), "Biography of Anthony Horowitz."

56 Sarah Crompton, "I Knew that Alex Was Special From The Start."

57 Dennis Abrams's email interview with Anthony Horowitz, July 28, 2005.

58 Dennis Abrams's phone interview with Anthony Horowitz, August 31, 2005.

59 Kate Kellaway, "Boy's Own Hero."

60 "Biography of Anthony Horowitz."

61 Ibid.

62 Ibid.

63 Dennis Abrams's phone interview with Anthony Horowitz, August 31, 2005

64 "Biography of Anthony Horowitz."

65 Ibid.

66 Nicolette Jones, "A Schoolboy James Bond is Busy Saving the World."

67 Amanda Craig, "An Interview with Anthony Horowitz."

68 Alec, "An Interview with Anthony Horowitz."

69 Dennis Abrams's email interview with Anthony Horowitz, July 28, 2005.

70 Alec, "An Interview with Anthony Horowitz."

71 Ibid.

72 Ibid.

73 Ibid.

74 Ibid.

75 Amanda Craig, "An Interview with Anthony Horowitz."

76 Danuta Kean, "Anthony Horowitz talks to Danuta Kean about sick jokes."

77 Alec, "An Interview with Anthony Horowitz."

78 Danuta Kean, "Anthony Horowitz talks to Danuta Kean about sick jokes."

79 Ibid.

80 Ibid.

81 Alec, "An Interview with Anthony Horowitz."

82 Anthony Horowitz, *The Killing Joke* (London, UK: Orion, 2004), back cover.

83 "Author Talk: Anthony Horowitz," Teenreads.com, May 2005, *www.teenreads.com/authors/ au-horowitz- anthony.asp#talk0505.*

84 Ilene Cooper, *Booklist* (Chicago, IL: American Library Association, 2005).

85 Caroline Horn, "The Horror of Horowitz," May 19, 2005, *www.thebookseller.com/?pid= 84&did=15990.*

86 Dennis Abrams's email interview with Anthony Horowitz, July 28, 2005.

87 Caroline Horn, "The Horror of Horowitz."

88 Dennis Abrams's email interview with Anthony Horowitz, July 28, 2005.

89 Ibid.

90 Ibid.

91 Dennis Abrams's phone interview

with Anthony Horowitz,
August 31, 2005.

92 Ibid.

1955 Anthony Horowitz born, April 5.

1963–68 Attends Orley Farm preparatory school.

1968–73 Attends Rugby School.

1973 Lives in Australia, working as a "jackaroo;" travels from Singapore back to England.

1974–77 Attends University of York.

1979 First book, *Enter Frederick K. Bower*, published.

1983 Writes for television series, *Dramarama*—his first work as television writer.

1985 *The Kingfisher Book of Myths and Legends* published.

1986 Begins work on *Robin of Sherwood* television series. First Diamond Brothers book, *The Falcon's Malteser* published, five additional titles follow.

1988 Marries Jill Green. *Groosham Grange* published.

1989 Birth of eldest son, Nicholas Horowitz. Begins work on *Poirot* television series. Success as a television writer allows him to stop working at McCann Erickson.

1991 Second son, Cassian Horowitz, born. *Return to Groosham Grange*, sequel to *Groosham Grange*, published.

1994 *Granny* published.

1996 *The Switch* published.

1997 Begins work on television series, *Midsomer Murders*.

2000 *Mindgame* opens on London's West End, but closes after only five weeks. *Stormbreaker*, the first in the highly popular Alex Rider series, published.

2002 *Foyle's War*, Anthony's most successful television series to date, debuts.

2005 Latest Alex Rider novel, *Ark Angel* published in the United Kingdom. Filming of *Stormbreaker* based on Anthony's screenplay begins.

ALEX RIDER SERIES

Stormbreaker, *Point Blank*, *Skeleton Key*, *Eagle Strike*, *Scorpia*, and *Ark Angel* are all books in Anthony Horowitz's most popular series featuring Alex Rider, teenage spy. After the death of his uncle and guardian Ian, Alex finds himself dragged into the shadow world of British Intelligence, working for M16. In one thrilling adventure after another, Alex steps in where adults cannot and saves the world again and again from a series of criminal masterminds.

THE DIAMOND BROTHERS SERIES

The Falcon's Malteser, *Public Enemy Number Two*, *South by South East*, *I Know What You Did Last Wednesday*, *The Blurred Man*, and *The French Confection* are the books that make up Anthony Horowitz's series of detective stories about two private investigators, Herbert "Nick" Diamond and his younger brother Tim (who is really the brains of the operation). Many of the plots in this series are take-offs on old movies and the series itself is a satirical and funny look at classic detective stories.

GRANNY

Anthony Horowitz takes an over-the-top look at his own grandmother in this funny horror story. Granny is a mean, ugly old woman who plots with a group of other grandmothers to steal her grandson Joe's enzymes, in an effort to make themselves young again.

GROOSHAM GRANGE AND RETURN TO GROOSHAM GRANGE

Written 10 years before Harry Potter appeared in children's books, these books follow the adventures of David Elliot, the seventh son of a seventh son, as he is sent to Groosham Grange, England's leading academy of witchcraft. It is here that David learns his destiny.

THE SWITCH

Tad Spencer, the son of a wealth British businessman, wishes on a star that he could be somebody else. The next morning he wakes up as Bob Snarby, living in a cheap carnival, surrounded by criminals and fortunetellers, while the real Bob Snarby is now living as Tad Spencer! How can Tad get back to his real life? Will he even want to?

1979   *Enter Frederick K. Bower*

1981   *The Devil's Door-Bell*

1984   *The Night of the Scorpion*

1985   *The Kingfisher Book of Myths and Legend*

1986   *Adventurer*

1986   *The Silver Citadel*

1986   *The Falcon's Malteser*

1987   *Robin of Sherwood: The Hooded Man*; *Public Enemy Number Two*

1988   *Groosham Grange*

1989   *Day of the Dragon*

1991   *Groosham Grange II: The Unholy Grail* (published in the United States as *Return to Groosham Grange*)

1994   *The Puffin Book of Horror Stories*; *Granny*

1996   *Death Walks Tonight: Horrifying Stories* (Editor and Contributor); *The Switch*

1998   *The Devil and His Boy*

1999   *Horowitz Horror: Nine nasty stories to chill you to the bone*

2000   *Mindgame*; *More Horowitz Horror: Eight sinister stories you'll wish you never read*; *Stormbreaker*

2001   *Point Blank*

2002   *Skeleton Key*; *I Know What You Did Last Wednesday*; *The Blurred Man*; *The French Confection*; *South by South East*

2003   *Eagle Strike*

2004   *Scorpia*; *The Killing Joke*

2005   *Ark Angel*; *Raven's Gate*

2006   *Evil Star*

HERBERT "TIM" DIAMOND AND NICK DIAMOND

When 13-year-old Nick Diamond's parents decide to mote from London to Australia, he decides he would rather live with his 23-year-old brother Tim, a former policeman now working as a private investigator. Unfortunately, Tim is not very smart and is probably the worst detective in the world. Fortunately, Nick has enough brains for the both of them. Together, they solve a series of humorous mysteries, largely based on classic movies.

IVY KETTLE

Ivy "Granny" Kettle, grandmother to Joe Warden, is an extraordinarily mean, nasty, ugly old lady, who tried to kill her own grandson in an attempt to become young again.

ALEX RIDER

Alex Rider is a 14-year-old orphan being raised by his guardian, Uncle Ian. After Uncle Ian is killed in what is called an automobile accident, Alex discovers that his uncle was in fact murdered, and almost ends up getting killed himself. Alex learns that his uncle had been working for the M16 British intelligence agency, and in order to stay alive, Alex joins the agency himself. With his intelligence and courage, and armed with great spy gadgets, Alex manages to save the world over and over again.

2001   *Stormbreaker* receives Stockport Children's Book Award.

2002   *Point Blank* receives Askew's Children's Book Award. *Skeleton Key* receives Calderdale Children's Book of the Year.

2002–03   *Point Blank* appears on the Texas Lone Star Reading List.

2003   *Skeleton Key* receives Red House Children's Book Award. *Stormbreaker* receives West Sussex Children's Book of the Year and Golden Archer Winner (Wisconsin).

2003–04   *Stormbreaker* receives Beehive Winner (Utah, Young Adult Category). *Point Blank* receives Maryland Black-Eyed Susan Book Award Winner.

2004   *Eagle Strike* receives Portsmouth Book Award. *Skeleton Key* receives ALA Quick Pick for Reluctant Readers and IRA-CBA Children's Choice. *Stormbreaker* receives Rebecca Caudill Award Winner (Illinois).

2004–05   *Stormbreaker* receives California Young Reader Medal Winner (Young Adult Category). *Skeleton Key* appears on the Texas Lone Star Reading List.

2005   *Scorpia* receives Berkshire Book Award and Staffordshire Young Teen Fiction Award. *Stormbreaker* receives Iowa Teen Award Winner. *Eagle Strike* receives ALA Best Book for Young Adults, ALA Quick Pick for Reluctant Readers, and New York Public Book for the Teen Age Reader.

Alec, "An interview with Anthony Horowitz," *Write Away! Meets Anthony Horowitz, http://improbability.ultralab.net/writeaway/anthony-horowitz.htm.*

"Author Talk: Anthony Horowitz," Teenreads.com, May 2005, *www.teen-reads.com/authors/au-horowitz-anthony.asp#talk0505.*

"Background about Crime Traveller," The Crime Traveller Homepage, *www.crimetraveller.co.uk/background.asp?css=yonb.*

"Biography of Anthony Horowitz." *Contemporary Authors.* Farmington Hills, MI: Thomson Gale, 2004.

Crompton, Sarah. "I Knew that Alex Was Special From The Start." *The Telegraph*, March 30, 2005.

Cooper, Ilene. *Booklist*, Chicago, IL: American Library Association, 2005.

Craig, Amanda. "An Interview with Anthony Horowitz." *www.amandacraig.com/pages/journalism/interviews/anthony_horowitz.htm.*

Forshaw, Barry. "Anthony Horowitz: Growing up in public." *The Independent*, August 13, 2004.

Horn, Caroline. "The Horror of Horowitz." May 19, 2005, *www.thebookseller.com/?pid=84&did=15990.*

Horowitz, Anthony. "Alex Rider: Frequently Asked Questions." *www.anthonyhorowitz.com/alexrider/faq/index.html.*

———. *The Devil and His Boy*. New York, NY: Philomel Books, 2000.

———. *Eagle Strike*, New York, NY: Philomel Books, 2005.

———. *Granny*. London, UK: Walker Books Ltd., 2004.

———. *Groosham Grange*. London, UK: Walker Books Ltd., 2003.

———. *The Killing Joke*. London, UK: Orion, 2004.

———. "Perils of Privilege." *Evening Standard*, March 24, 2003.

———. *Public Enemy Number Two*. New York, NY: Puffin Books, 2004.

———. *Stormbreaker*. New York, NY: Philomel Books, 2004.

———. *The Switch*. London, UK: Walker Books Ltd., 2004.

———. *Three of Diamonds*. New York, NY: Puffin Books, 2005.

Jones, Nicolette. "A Schoolboy James Bond is Busy Saving the World." *The Times* (of London), September 11, 2001.

Kean, Danuta. "Anthony Horowitz talks to Danuta Kean about sick jokes." *www.orionbooks.co.uk/interview.aspx?ID=10964.*

Kellaway, Kate. "Boy's Own Hero." *The Guardian*, April 10, 2005.

Kirkus Reviews, "Review of The Devil and His Boy." New York, NY: Kirkus Associates, L.P., 1999, *www.amazon.com/gp/product/product-*

*description/0698119134/ref=dp_proddesc_0/103-5847675-
1779802?%5Fencoding=UTF8&n=283155.*

"Mindgame on stage in London's West End Vaudeville Theatre," *London
Theatre Guide*, *www.albemarle-london.com/mindgame.html.*

Penguin Group (Canada). "Biography of Anthony Horowitz." Penguin
Books Authors.
www.penguin.ca/nf/Author/AuthorPage/0,,0_1000015379,00.html.

Scotto, Barbara. "Review of The Devil and His Boy." *School Library
Journal*. New York, NY: Reed Business Information, Inc., 2000.

Weisman, Kate. *Booklist*, Chicago, IL: American Library Association,
2004.

Dahl, Roald. *The Witches*. New York, NY: Puffin Books, 1998.

Dickens, Charles. *Great Expectations*. New York, NY: Penguin Classics, 2002.

Fleming, Ian. *From Russia with Love*. New York, NY: Penguin, 2002.

Horowitz, Anthony. *The Falcon's Malteser*. New York, NY: Puffin Books, 2004.

————. *Horowitz Horror: Nine nasty stories to chill you to the bone*. London, UK: Orchard Books, 1999.

————. *More Horowitz Horror: Eight sinister stories you'll wish you'd never read*. London, UK: Orchard Books, 2000.

————. *Point Blank*, New York, NY: Speak, 2004.

————. *Return to Groosham Grange*. London, UK: Walker Books Ltd., 2003.

————. *Skeleton Key*. New York, NY: Speak, 2004.

————. *Scorpia*. New York, NY: Philomel Books, 2005.

www.anthonyhorowitz.com

This is the official website for Anthony Horowitz. It includes all things Anthony, including news, contact links, and updates on upcoming works.

www.amazon.uk.co

This is the best source for many of Anthony Horowitz's books that are not yet published in the United States.

page:

10:	© Getty Images	44:	© Orley Farm School
15:	© Bettmann/CORBIS	49:	© Barclay Graham/COR-BIS SYGMA
16:	© 21st Century Publishing	76:	© Des Willie, 2003
25:	© Hulton-Deutsch Collection/CORBIS	84:	© Chelsea House Publishers
28:	Courtesy of Stuart Hill	96:	Courtesy of Dulwich College
31:	© Chelsea House Publishers	99:	Courtesy of Vertigo Theatre Factory
36:	© Chelsea House Publishers		
42:	© John Springer Collection/CORBIS		

Cover: Des Willie, 2003

DENNIS ABRAMS attended Antioch College, where he majored in English and Communications. A voracious reader since the age of three, Dennis is a freelance writer in Houston, Texas, where he lives with his partner of eighteen years, along with their two dogs and three cats.